HTML
MANUAL OF STYLE

HTML
Manual of Style

Ziff-Davis Press
Emeryville, California

Larry Aronson

Copy Editor	Kelly Green
Technical Reviewer	Clay Shirky
Project Coordinator	Ami Knox
Proofreaders	Ami Knox and Barbara Dahl
Cover Illustration	Regan Honda
Cover Design	Regan Honda
Book Design	Gary Suen
Screen Graphics Editor	Pipi Diamond
Word Processing	Howard Blechman
Page Layout	Tony Jonick
Indexer	Carol Burbo

Ziff-Davis Press books are produced on a Macintosh computer system with the following applications: FrameMaker®, Microsoft® Word, QuarkXPress®, Adobe Illustrator®, Adobe Photoshop®, Adobe Streamline™, MacLink®*Plus*, Aldus® FreeHand™, Collage Plus™.

If you have comments or questions or would like to receive a free catalog, call or write:
Ziff-Davis Press
5903 Christie Avenue
Emeryville, CA 94608
1-800-688-0448

ISBN 1-56276-300-8

Manufactured in the United States of America
10 9 8 7 6 5 4

TABLE OF CONTENTS

ACKNOWLEDGEMENTS

I'd like to thank all the people who helped me write this book. At ZD Press, I'd especially like to thank Clay Shirky and Eric Stone, who got me involved in this project; and Kelly Green and Ami Knox, who have done a fantastic job editing the manuscript and moving the book through production. I'd also like to thank the people who gave permission to display their works in the examples section and the many others who provided feedback and advice. A big special thank-you hug goes to my best friend, Lynne Thigpen, for her help and encouragement. Finally, I'd like to acknowledge my deep debt of gratitude to the many people who continually sustain the Web by writing documentation and software tools and by participating in the WWW and HTML discussion groups.

INTRODUCTION

During the past year a revolution has been happening over our world's telecommunications networks. It's called the World Wide Web, and its growth has been nothing less than phenomenal. Of course, no revolution comes out of nowhere, and so it is with the World Wide Web. Developments, both technological and social, have paved the way for the emergence of the Web. Computers, once confined only to those who could master the arcane mysteries of programming languages, are now part of the everyday world of businesspeople, artists, and schoolchildren. The Internet, a set of protocols that permitted universities and other large organizations to exchange data, has now become the hottest trend of the nineties. The World Wide Web ties the two together, breaking the physical barriers of Cyberspace to establish the foundation of a global electronic village.

The World Wide Web provides a means of accessing the resources of the Internet without requiring the user to know how those resources are transmitted and stored. The Web's hypermedia paradigm expands the potential of the Internet and empowers technical and nontechnical people alike with a simple, low-cost method of providing information, opinions, and art to a world-wide audience of millions. This book is about harnessing that power. It is a "lean and mean" instructional guide to HTML, the HyperText Markup Language that is the lingua franca of the Web. In this slim volume lies the means by which you can join the revolution, not as just a passive consumer of information, but as a publisher of information.

This book is primarily for those who are already exploring the Web with programs such as Lynx and Mosaic and who now wish to put their own information out there for others to utilize. Don't fret if you're not there yet. These programs are available for most computer platforms and, in most cases, are free. Getting an Internet connection used to be rather difficult. Now, however, on the same bookshelf where this book can be found, you will find all-in-one kits that will get you connected to the Internet and surfing the Web in a matter of hours. HTML is very easy to learn. You do not need any prior experience with programming languages: A familiarity with any modern word processing program will suffice. Since the World Wide Web encompasses most of the other protocols of the Internet, some knowledge of basic Internet procedures, such as e-mail, ftp, gopher, and newsgroups, will be helpful; however, such knowledge is not required to understand how the Web works and how to publish information on it.

This book consists of four chapters and three appendixes. Chapter 1 provides an introduction to HTML, the basic concepts of hypertext and hypermedia, the World Wide Web, and the Internet. Chapter 2 explains the structure and syntax of HTML and covers the details of the various elements of the language. Chapter 3 provides a discussion of proper HTML style and shows how to build good hypertext documents. Chapter 4 is a collection of World Wide Web pages and the complete HTML sources that generate them. Appendix A provides a quick reference to HTML; Appendix B shows a preview of the next generation of the language HTML+; and Appendix C is a resource guide.

This book was created and edited on an ancient (six-year-old) Apple Macintosh II computer and a more recent Macintosh PowerBook 160 using Microsoft Word version 5.1. Manuscript pages were printed on an Apple Personal Laser-Writer NTR printer. For research, I used several World Wide Web browsers— NCSA Mosaic (versions 1.0.3 and 2.0A8), MacWeb (version 1.00A2.2), Netscape (version 0.9b), and Enhanced NCSA Mosaic (version 1.01). My connection to the Internet is via a dialup PPP (Point-to-Point Protocol) link to Panix, a local Internet service provider, using a Zoom Technologies V.32bis modem.

This is my first book. I welcome your comments, suggestions and criticism. Please send them to me via e-mail at: laronson@acm.org. Thanks, and enjoy.

Larry Aronson
New York City

What Is HTML?

HTML: A STANDARD GENERALIZED
MARKUP LANGUAGE

HYPERTEXT AND HYPERMEDIA

MOSAIC, THE WORLD WIDE WEB, AND THE
INTERNET

Chapter

1

Hypertext Markup Language (HTML) is a system for marking up documents with informational tags that indicate how text in the documents should be presented and how the documents are linked together. Hypertext links are quite powerful. Within the HTML markup scheme lies the power to create interactive, cross-platform, multimedia, client-server applications. This string of adjectives is not just hype; such systems do exist. One, called the World Wide Web (WWW), lives on the Internet, providing organization to a wide variety of resources on computers located around the globe. The Web, also known as WWW or W3, plays a large part in the continuing development of HTML, and the Web will play a large part in the way you write and structure HTML documents. The World Wide Web represents the largest possible audience for your work.

HTML: A STANDARD GENERALIZED MARKUP LANGUAGE

HTML is not a programming language and an HTML document is not a computer program. It's a lot simpler than that. A computer program is a series of procedures and instructions applied, typically, to external data. An HTML document, however, *is* the data. The HTML language specifies the grammar and syntax of markup tags that, when inserted into the data, tell *browsers*—computer programs that read HTML documents, such as NCSA Mosaic—how to present the document. Technically, HTML is defined as a Standard Generalized

Markup Language (SGML), Document Type Definition (DTD). An HTML document is said to be an *instance* of a SGML document.

SGML originated as GML (General Markup Language) at IBM in the late sixties as an attempt to solve some of the problems of transporting documents across different computer systems. The term *markup* comes from the publishing industry, where it refers to the coded typesetting instructions inserted into a manuscript by an editor. SGML is *generalized*, meaning that instead of specifying exactly how to present a document, it describes document types, along with markup languages to format and present instances of each type. GML became SGML when it was accepted as a *standard* by the International Standards Organization (ISO) in Geneva, Switzerland (reference number ISO 8879:1986).

A SGML document has three parts. The first describes the character set and, most importantly, which characters are used to differentiate the text from the markup tags. The second part declares the document type and which markup tags are accepted as legal. The third part is called the document instance and contains the actual text and the markup tags. The three parts need not be in the same physical file, which is a good thing because it allows us to forget about SGML and deal only with HTML. All HTML browsers assume the same information for the SGML character-set and document-type declarations, so we only have to work with HTML document instances—simple text files.

The base character set of an HTML document is ISO 8859/1, also known as Latin-1. It's an 8-bit alphabet with characters for most American and European languages. ISO 646, also known as ASCII, is a 7-bit subset of Latin-1. There is no obligation to use anything but the 128 standard ASCII characters in an HTML document. In fact, sticking to straight ASCII is encouraged as it allows an HTML document to be edited by any text editor on any computer system and be transported over any network by even the most rudimentary of e-mail and file transfer systems. To make this possible, HTML includes character entities for most of the commonly used non-ASCII Latin-1 characters. Character entities begin with the ampersand character (&), followed by the name or number of the character, followed by a semicolon. For example, the character entity for a small *e* with a grave accent (`) is &*egrave;*.

HTML markup tags are delimited by the angle brackets, < and >. They appear either singularly, like the tag *<P>* indicating a paragraph break in the text, or as a pair of starting and ending tags. *<B>Attention!</B>*, for example, is an instruction to present the text string *Attention!* in a bold typeface. There are tags for formatting text, tags for specifying hypertext links, tags for including sound and picture elements, and tags for defining input fields for interactive pages.

That's all there is to HyperText Markup Language—character entities and markup tags. However, this system of entities and tags is growing. There are currently several standardization levels of HTML.

Level 1 is the level mandatory for all WWW browsers. It is essentially what was accepted by the first browsers (level 0), plus images.

Level 2 includes all the elements of level 1, plus tags for defining user input fields. At the time of this writing, the SGML specification for level 2 is being finalized; this is mostly a matter of catching up with accepted practice as implemented in popular Web browsers.

Level 3, also known as HTML+, is currently in development. It includes markup tags for objects such as tables, figures, and mathematical equations.

The next chapter describes the HTML language, including most level 2 features.

Almost all of the development work on HTML is done on the World Wide Web in the form of discussions groups, which post proposed changes and issue requests for comments. The complete specifications of HTML (the SGML DTD) can always be found on the Web. The Web is also the place to look for the most up-to-date HTML and SGML documentation, most of it in hypertext. Appendix C has a listing of Web addresses for many of these documents.

HYPERTEXT AND HYPERMEDIA

What exactly is hypertext? Hypertext is text that is not constrained to be linear. In reading this book, for example, you may skip some chapters and make occasional trips to the appendixes. Still, it is, as presented to you, a linear sequence of pages. In contrast, hypertext organizes information as an interconnected web of linked text. Different paths can be followed through the work by different readers; readers can choose among all the links the authors provided those associations most relevant to their immediate needs. Hypermedia refers to hypertext applications that contain things other than text objects. *Hypermedia* applications encompass graphics, video, sound, and more. The HyperText Markup Language contains markup tags for specifying links to multimedia objects. How these objects are displayed is left up to the browser, but generally, pictures are expanded as illustrations or figures within the text, while sound and animation are presented in their own windows with stop and play controls.

On an HTML hypertext page, the highlighted text that serves as the start of a link is called an anchor. Anchors can be embedded in other HTML elements, which allows you to assemble and present lists of hypertext links. A picture can serve as the anchor for a link as well as text. Small pictures can be used as clickable icons and buttons on a Web page. This is especially useful when you want to create a standard set of controls that are placed on a series of Web pages. Images can also have multiple anchors attached to different areas of the image. In this way, interactive maps can be defined.

The wonderful thing about hypertext is that it adds an extra dimension of structure to the content of your work. With hypertext, you can highlight alternative relationships in the text besides the linear ordering of sections, chapters, and subchapters found in the table of contents. A hypertext work is bounded only by the physical storage space available for linked documents. For the World Wide Web and the Internet, this means terabytes of data, and the Web is growing faster than anyone could possibly keep up with. With the slick graphical browsers that have become available in the last year, you actually experience the sensation of "surfing" through an unbounded information space.

The concepts of hypertext and hypermedia have been around for a while; Ted Nelson is given credit for coining the terms in 1965. The first practical hypermedia application was the "Aspen Movie Map" done at MIT in 1978. It used videodisk and touch-screen technology. Filevision from Telos, released in 1984, gave hypermedia databases to early Macintosh users. In 1987, Apple introduced Hypercard, written by Bill Atkinson, which incorporated many hypermedia concepts. The development of CD-ROM drives for personal computers made the commercial development and marketing of multimedia applications a reality. And in 1989, Tim Berners-Lee and Robert Cailliau submitted a proposal to their colleagues at CERN for a client-server–based hypermedia system, and the World Wide Web was born.

HTML hypermedia applications are similar in many ways to Macintosh Hypercard applications; enough so that it's possible to mimic simple Hypercard applications in HTML and vice versa. Both systems take the form of a web of linked nodes with one node designated as home—the home stack for Hypercard and the home page for a World Wide Web server. The differences, however, are significant; not the least important is that Hypercard applications only run on Apple Macintosh computers, whereas HTML applications run on linked networks connecting a variety of different kinds of computers.

Hypercard uses the metaphor of a stack of cards containing layers of information objects (pictures and text fields) and buttons. Usually, cards are no larger than a computer screen and are presented one at a time. A button can have an attached script activated by a mouse click. Script actions typically are links to other cards or stacks. Hypertalk, the scripting language that drives Hypercard applications, is powerful, elegant, and fairly easy to learn.

The metaphor for HTML applications is that of a page of formatted text and pictures. An HTML page can be many physical pages long, corresponding to a chapter in a book or a section of a manual; however, the width is variable—the browser presenting the page word-wraps the text and positions the pictures to fit the width of the display window. HTML hypertext links are activated by clicking with a mouse button on highlighted text (usually underlined and displayed in a color different than is nonlinked text) or picture. The link may be to other text on the same page, to a new Web page, or to some other kind of resource on the network or the Internet. Whereas Hypercard's Hypertalk is most definitely a programming language, HTML is not. It is powerful and it is easy to learn, but I don't think many would call it elegant.

Another key difference between Hypercard and HTML/Web applications is that Hypercard is designed for a personal computer—you maintain your own copies of the stacks you access somewhere on your computer's hard disk or on the local area network. Hypercard is best at personal record–keeping applications; phone books and time logs, for example. HTML documents, on the other hand, exist in a client-server environment. The clients are the browsers. Servers are programs running on remote computers that provide Web pages and other files requested by browsers. Because HTML can link documents on servers located in remote parts of the world, HTML applications are more suited for organizing and serving relatively static information to a large public.

The next section will have more to say about browsers. A full discussion of servers, however, is beyond the scope of this book. Suffice it to say that most Web servers, but not all, are running on UNIX machines with high-speed connections to the Internet.

For an HTML application to be "on the Web" means that the HTML files and other documents that make up the application must reside in a directory that is accessible to a Web server. Note that this does not mean there must be a link from some existing Web page to your document in order for your document to be part of the Web. The Web assigns a unique address, called a Uniform Resource Locator (URL), for every resource it recognizes. There are URL formats for non-HTML objects on the Internet: Gophers, Wide Area Information Servers (WAIS), ftp archives, Newsgroups, and Telnet-able machines. Since most browsers have the ability to directly load a URL from the user, just about anything on the Internet is also on the World Wide Web.

MOSAIC, THE WORLD WIDE WEB, AND THE INTERNET

A lot has been written recently about the Internet, Mosaic, and the World Wide Web. What's all the excitement about? Is Mosaic the "killer app" of the '90s?

Well, it just might be. The first time you start exploring the Web with a graphical browser like Mosaic, you have the astonishing sensation of a myth turning into reality before your very eyes. The myth is the dream of a universal information database that science fiction writers have given us over the past half century. Today, with Mosaic and the World Wide Web, we indeed have a simple, easy-to-use interface to all the computerized information in the world—cyberspace at your fingertips.

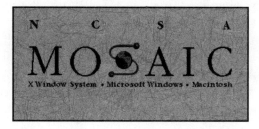

Mosaic is one of several browser programs that processes HTML documents on Web server networks. An up-to-date listing of browser software is usually available from a link on the World Wide Web home page at CERN, http://info.cern.ch/hypertext/WWW/Clients.html. Mosaic is the premier browser, and gets most of the press, largely because it was the first graphical browser for the Web and because it exists in versions for Macintosh, Windows, and UNIX/X-Windows systems. Mosaic's popularity is not at all diminished by the fact that it's free. It was developed with U.S. tax dollars by the National Center for Supercomputing Activities (NCSA) at the University of Illinois in Urbana, home of the HAL 9000.

This book uses NCSA Mosaic for the Macintosh, version 2.0.0, for screen shots and examples of formatted HTML documents. The results will look much the same for Mosaic's Windows and UNIX versions using the default preferences for fonts and styles. The examples should also produce similar results for other graphical browsers like MacWeb for Macintosh and Cello for Windows. NCSA is licensing Mosaic technology to several corporations, so by the time you read this, there may be commercial versions available with built-in WYSIWYG editing and other neat features. In the meantime, you can get Mosaic from NCSA's anonymous ftp server, ftp://ftp.ncsa.uiuc.edu/Web/Mosaic/, as well as from many commercial online services, including ZiffNet.

Besides graphical Web browsers, there are also *linemode* browsers, which can be used to browse the Web via Telnet and dial-up BBSs. Probably the most popular of these is Lynx from the University of Kansas, which makes use of the feature set of a DEC VT-100, a common display terminal that's emulated by most telecommunications software. Cursor keys are used instead of a mouse to select and activate links. The important difference between graphical and linemode browsers is that graphical browsers run on your personal computer and can make full use of your operating system's toolbox, whereas linemode browsers run on somebody else's computer, to which you are connected as a remote terminal.

In order to run Mosaic or any other graphical browser, your computer must be part of the Internet. This is not as big a deal as it sounds. It means that your computer has to run some form of the Internet's networking software, TCP/IP; and if your machine is not connected to a network with an Internet gateway, you also need modem software, either a Serial Line Interface Protocol (SLIP) driver or a Point to Point Protocol (PPP) driver. These drivers run at the operating-system level of your computer, allowing Mosaic and other Internet client applications—e-mail, gopher, and Telnet for example—to run concurrently, each in their own window. TCP/IP (Transmission Control Protocol/Internet Protocol) takes the information from the client applications and formats it into data packets with Internet addressing, then passes the packets to the modem driver, which sends them out your modem and phone line to an Internet gateway. Gateways are provided by Internet service providers, who will give you a SLIP or PPP account on either an hourly or flat-fee basis. Flat-fee accounts run about $35 per month.

Mosaic can access documents locally—in other words, you can implement an HTML application on your own local area network and not be connected to the Internet at all. For your application to be part of the World Wide Web, however, your documents must be accessible to a Web server. You can run your own server: The software is available for a number of machines—the CERN and NCSA versions are free—but it's better to find space on someone else's Web server. If your organization is already running an Internet server—gopher, for example—chances are that it has, or is considering, setting up a World Wide Web server as well.

World Wide Web Initiative

Is the World Wide Web the same thing as the Internet? Well, yes and no. The Internet is physically much bigger than the Web; there are still more Gopher servers than Web servers, for example. Yet everything on the Internet can be addressed by a Web link, so in a way, the Web is the Internet seen from a different point of view; one not tied down to the physical hardware.

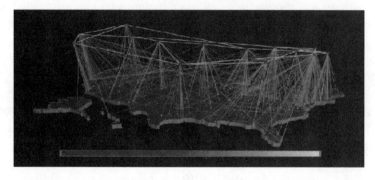

The Internet started in the late 1960s as a U.S. Department of Defense project linking together universities' and military research institutes' computers. In the early 1980s the military bowed out and got its own network; the rest was given to the National Science Foundation (someone had to run the actual hardware); but in reality, no one owns or runs the Internet. It is the largest functioning anarchy in the world. In the last few years, Internet growth has been explosive. New networks are connected via gateways to the Internet on a daily basis. In the past year, scores of new Internet service providers have come on line, providing low-cost connections for the general public. Hypertext has turned out to be an ideal way to organize the diverse resources of the Internet. The World Wide Web has arrived just in time.

The HTML Language

HTML SYNTAX

FORMATTING TAGS

ANCHORS AND LINKS

IMAGES

FORMS

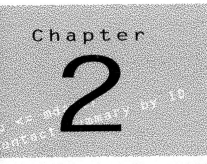

Chapter

2

This chapter presents the various elements of the HTML language — the syntax of character entities and markup tags and how they are interpreted by a browser to display a page. This description corresponds to the just finalized HTML level 2 specification and, therefore, these elements should be recognized by most graphical browsers that are now available and those that will be available in the future as HTML technology continues to evolve. A few companies have already put out browsers that go beyond the HTML level 2 specification with tags for special formatting and style control. There is an on-going debate at conferences and via e-mail over these features and how to best extend the language for all browsers without sacrificing its simplicity. While it is not practical to address here all the possible directions the language will take, the material that is provided in this chapter is sufficient for presenting your information in a professional and attractive manner.

HTML SYNTAX

There are only a few general syntax rules to learn in constructing Web documents in HTML. Every HTML document or page is divided into two parts, a head and a body. The *head* contains information about the document and the *body* contains the text of the document. Markup tags are used to define the two parts, as in this minimal HTML page:

```
<HEAD>
<TITLE>Minimal HTML Page</TITLE>
</HEAD>
```

```
<BODY>
Text, possibly with embedded HTML elements.
</BODY>
```

In this example, the only information specified in the head of the document is the document's title. This is all you will usually find in the document's head. Certain other informational tags can go there, but they represent advanced features that may or may not be supported by your Web server. The body of the document, in this example, contains one paragraph of text. It looks like one line of text, but formally, we call it a paragraph because it's possible that some reader running a browser in a narrow display window on her PC will see that text word-wrap into multiple lines. The term *lines* has meaning only in the context of pre-formatted text, a markup style that preserves line breaks and white space. Otherwise, a paragraph of text is word-wrapped to fit the width of the reader's display in the same way as paragraph text is wrapped in most word processing programs.

Every HTML document or page should have a title; preferably a short one that's meaningful in the larger context of the work. With most browsers, the title appears either as the title of the display window or at the top of that window. Titles are not absolutely required; many text documents on the Web are simply text files, containing no markup elements and having no titles. Mosaic and most other browsers are quite forgiving and will allow you to omit the head and body tags, although it's a good idea to keep them in.

There are two kinds of HTML elements; character entities and markup tags. A *character entity* begins with an ampersand (&), followed either by the name of a predefined entity or a pound sign, followed by the decimal number of the character, and, finally, by a semicolon to terminate the character entity. The tilde (~), for example, can be generated by the sequence *~*.

Many character entities are predefined for the purpose of placing special characters into the text, such as characters from the ISO Latin-1 alphabet that are not defined in ASCII, and characters that are needed to define HTML elements. A complete list of HTML level 2 predefined character entities can be found in Appendix A. Some of the more useful are:

<   Left angle bracket or less-than sign

>   Right angle bracket or greater-than sign

&   Ampersand

Also useful are:

"   Double quote mark

     Nonbreaking space

Every markup tag has a tag ID (or name) and possibly some attributes. Markup tags are either empty or nonempty. *Nonempty* tags act upon text enclosed in a pair of starting and ending tags. A starting tag begins with the left angle bracket (<) followed immediately by the tag ID, any attributes, then the right angle bracket (>) to close the tag. Ending tags are exactly the same except that there is a slash (/) immediately between the opening bracket and the tag ID and ending tags cannot contain any attributes. If the tag is an *empty* tag, then there is no enclosed text and the ending tag is omitted. Here are some examples of empty tags:

<P>   Begin a new paragraph

<HR>   Insert a horizontal rule

The following empty tag specifies that an in-line image be inserted. It has one attribute, the SRC attribute, whose value is the name (source) of the file containing the image:

```
<IMG SRC="company_logo.gif">
```

Attributes take the form of NAME=VALUE, where the value is appropriate to the domain of the attribute. The value should be enclosed in double quotes, although it's safe to drop the quotes when the value is a simple number or name. If there's more than one attribute in a tag, they are separated by blanks, not commas. Some attributes can take the same value as the name of the attribute. In these cases, the attribute can be written in an abbreviated form, for example:

```
"<DL COMPACT>" for <DL COMPACT="COMPACT">
```

Here are some examples of nonempty tags:

```
<TITLE>Don Quixote</TITLE>
<I>This should appear in italics</I>
<TT>Fixed width, typewriter font</TT>
<A HREF="catalog.html">our current catalog</A>
```

The last example above is an anchor. *Anchors* are tags that define the nodes of hypertext links. In this example, the phrase *our current catalog* will be highlighted by the browser to show that it is a link. Clicking on it (or selecting it if you're using a nongraphical browser) will instruct the browser to load the next hypertext page from the file *catalog.html*, specified as the value of the HREF (Hypertext REFerence) attribute. (See "Anchors and Links" later in this chapter for more on anchors and hypertext addressing formats.)

Here's a simple example illustrating the use of markup tags and character entities:

```
<HEAD>
<TITLE>Simple HTML Example</TITLE>
</HEAD>

<BODY>
<H1>Level 1 Headings</H1>

Whereas <STRONG>Titles</STRONG> should have some
relation to the outside world, Level 1 Headings
should introduce the major sections of the work.
<P>
This is a second paragraph of text inserted to show
how paragraph tags are used to separate text and to
point out the use of the &lt;STRONG&gt; tag in the
first paragraph.
</BODY>
```

Figure 2.1 shows what this example looks like on a Macintosh using Mosaic with the default preferences set.

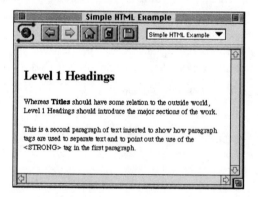

Figure 2.1: Titles and headings in HTML.

First off, note that the title of the page, *Simple HTML Example*, appears as the window title. The body of this example page consists of a level 1 heading marked with the <H1> and </H1> tags, and two paragraphs of text separated by the paragraph tag, <P>. You can also see how Mosaic has ignored the carriage returns placed in the HTML page and word-wrapped the text to fit the width of its window.

In the second paragraph, in order to get the string <STRONG> to appear without being interpreted as a tag, character entities are used—*<* for the less-than sign (<), and *>* for the greater-than sign (>).

Although the HTML text in this example is neatly formatted, it doesn't actually matter where the tags are placed with respect to the page. The following HTML segments will all produce the exact same result as in the above illustration:

```
<H1>Level 1 Headings</H1>
```

```
<h1>
Level 1 Headings
</h1>
```

```
<H1>Level 1
Headings</h1 >
```

That's right! Tag IDs are not case sensitive. You can freely mix upper- and lowercase letters. White space—redundant blanks, tabs, line feeds, carriage returns, and most other ASCII control characters—is only allowed after the tag ID and before the closing bracket; in other words, the string

```
< H1 >Wrong, Wrong, Wrong!< /H1 >
```

will not be processed as a heading. The brackets and their contents will be ignored and only the enclosed text, W*rong, Wrong, Wrong!*, will appear. This is the standard procedure browsers follow for most errors—they ignore them. If an anchor tag is correct but the link is in error, then Mosaic and other browsers will return a status message such as *Unable to connect to remote host* or *Unable to access document.*

Tags usually can be nested—for example, anchors inside of list structures. However, some nestings are not allowed—for example, anchors inside of other anchors or a heading inside preformatted text. Other nestings are allowed but discouraged—for example, using a list structure inside a heading or combining style tags. The following two tag structures, applying emphasis and italics to text, may or may not display equally, depending on the browser.

```
<EM>Important news with a <I>slant</I></EM>
<EM>Important news with a </EM><I>slant</I>
```

You can place comments in an HTML document to annotate your work just as you would with other computer languages. Comments are completely ignored by the browser. An HTML comment is actually a SGML comment. It starts with the string <!--, can contain any character, and ends with the first occurrence of the string -->. As a general rule, place each comment on a separate line and avoid using any of the special characters, like <, >, &, or !. Some older browsers may not parse the comment correctly. Comments cannot be nested.

FORMATTING TAGS

HTML formatting tags can be divided into two loose classes—those that provide structure to the text of a page and those that change the style of the text. Into the structure class go headings, paragraphs, and lists. Into the style class go tags for adding emphasis and designating font styles. The classes are loose in the sense that some structure tags—headings, for example—imply whatever font changes are necessary to set off the heading from the rest of the text; and some style tags—blockquote, for example—imply a paragraph break before and after the marked-up text.

HEADINGS

HTML supports six levels of headings, designated by the tags <H1>, <H2>, <H3>, <H4>, <H5>, and <H6>. This is sufficient for most hypertext applications, because much of the structure of a hypertext work is in the web of links and additional structure can be generated by using the various list structures.

H1 is the highest level of heading, and it is customary to place a level 1 heading as the first element in the body of the document. A heading element implies a style change, including a paragraph break before and after the heading, and whatever white space is needed to render a heading of that level. Adding style tags to a heading or inserting paragraph tags to set off the heading is neither required nor recommended.

Headings should be used in their natural hierarchical order, as in an outline. Although it is legal to skip heading levels—to follow an H1 with an H3, for example—it is not recommended as it may produce strange results when processing the document with a parser other than an HTML browser. Here is an HTML page illustrating the six different heading levels:

```
<HEAD>
<TITLE>Heading Levels</TITLE>
</HEAD>

<BODY>
<H1>Level 1 Heading</H1>
First paragraph of text.
<H2>Level 2 Heading</H2>
Second paragraph of text.
<H3>Level 3 Heading</H3>
Third paragraph of text.
```

```
<H4>Level 4 Heading</H4>
Fourth paragraph of text.
<H5>Level 5 Heading</H5>
Fifth paragraph of text.
<H6>Level 6 Heading</H6>
Sixth paragraph of text.
</BODY>
```

Figure 2.2 shows how these headings will appear in Mosaic.

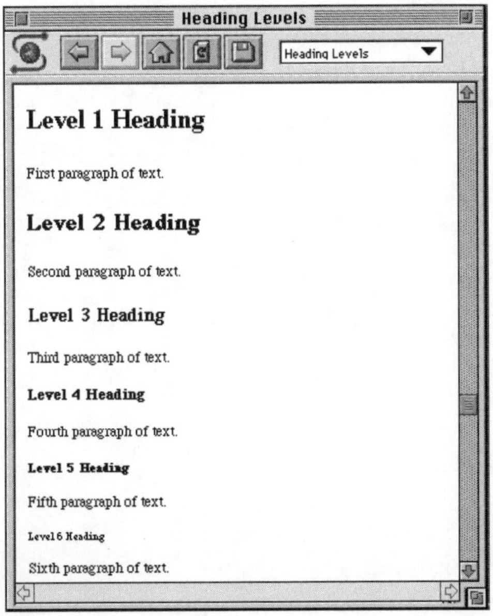

Figure 2.2: The six HTML heading levels

Different browsers may format the HTML page differently than Mosaic does, but the general look and feel of the formatted page should be the same as the above example for all graphical browsers.

PARAGRAPHS

As mentioned above, carriage returns, tabs, and other white space are ignored by the browser. To mark the beginning of a new paragraph on an HTML page, you must use the paragraph tag, <P>. The paragraph tag is empty—that is, there is no corresponding end tag. Paragraphs may or may not appear indented; that's up to the browser. Most browsers do insert extra white space to separate a paragraph from the previous one.

The line break tag, <BR>, is similar to the paragraph tag, but simpler. It forces the text directly following the tag onto the next line at the left margin (relative to any enclosing tags such as lists) without the addition of any white space.

Another way of separating blocks of text is with a line drawn across the width of the page. This is called a horizontal rule, and the tag for it is <HR>. This is a nice feature, as the browser will adjust the length of the line to fit the width of the displayed page. The following example has paragraph, line break, and horizontal rule tags.

```
<HEAD>
<TITLE>Paragraphs and Line Breaks</TITLE>
</HEAD>

<BODY>
<H1>Twelve</H1>
<HR>
The five colors blind the eye.<BR>
The five tones deafen the ear.<BR>
The five flavors dull the taste.<BR>
Racing and hunting madden the mind.<BR>
Precious things lead one astray.
<P>
Therefore the sage is guided by what he feels and not by what he sees.<BR>
He lets go of that and chooses this.
<HR>
</BODY>
```

Figure 2.3 shows this example.

LISTS

HTML supports several types of list structures that can be used in a document. A *list* is defined as a sequence of paragraphs, each marked with the list item tag, <LI>. The entire sequence of list items is enclosed with the starting and ending tags appropriate to the kind of list. These are:

<OL></OL>	An ordered list, typically indented with extra line spacing between numbered paragraphs
<UL></UL>	An unordered list; like an ordered list but with bullets instead of numbers
<MENU></MENU>	A list of short items, usually one line apiece, rendered more compactly than <UL>
<DIR></DIR>	A list of very short elements, such as file names, possibly rendered in multiple columns

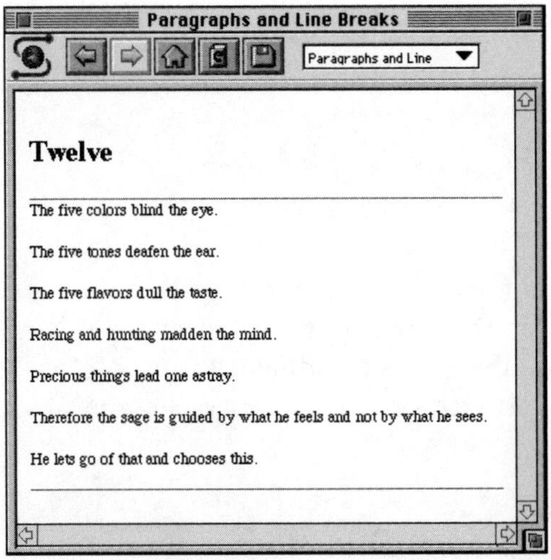

Figure 2.3: HTML paragraphs and line breaks

Like headings, there are implied paragraph marks before and after a list. Lists can be nested, making them ideal for implementing outlines and tables of contents. Here's an example using ordered, unordered, and menu lists:

```
<HEAD>
<TITLE>Examples of Lists</TITLE>
</HEAD>
<BODY>
<H1>HTML Book</H1>
<HR>
<!--Use headings for major sections-->
<H2>Table of Contents</H2>
<H3>Chapters</H3>
<OL>
<LI>Introduction
<LI>The Language
<!--Use bullets for the next level-->
    <UL>
    <LI>Syntax
    <LI>Formatting
    </UL>
<LI>Writing Documents
</OL>
<!--Use a menu for the Appendix-->
```

```
<H3>Appendix</H3>
<MENU>
<LI>Appendix A
</MENU>
<HR>
<!-- Oops, Mustn't forget to sign my work -->
<I>L.Aronson</I> &lt;laronson@acm.org&gt;
</BODY>
```

The indentations in the text above are only there to make the HTML easier to read; in no way do they affect how Mosaic or any other browser formats the text. Notice that there are no ending list tags (</LI>). You can put them in but they will be ignored by most browsers. Figure 2.4 shows how the example looks.

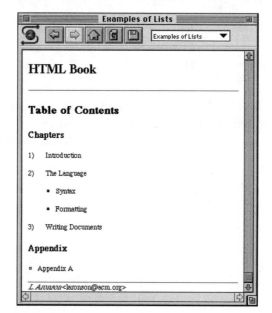

Figure 2.4: Using HTML lists

There's another kind of list called a definition list or glossary. It is a list of paragraphs each of which has a short title. This is useful for presenting a list of named items to the reader, each with an accompanying paragraph of definition or explanation. The entire definition list is enclosed with the tags <DL>

and </DL>. Each definition list item is composed of a term and definition pair as in the following example:

```
<H2>Cast of Characters</H2>
<DL>
<DT>Orsino <DD>Duke of Illyria.
<DT>Sebastian <DD>Brother to Viola.
<DT>Antonio <DD>A sea captain, friend to Sebastian.
<DT>Fabian <DD>A pop star of the early sixties.
</DL>
```

Figure 2.5 shows how this example looks on the screen.

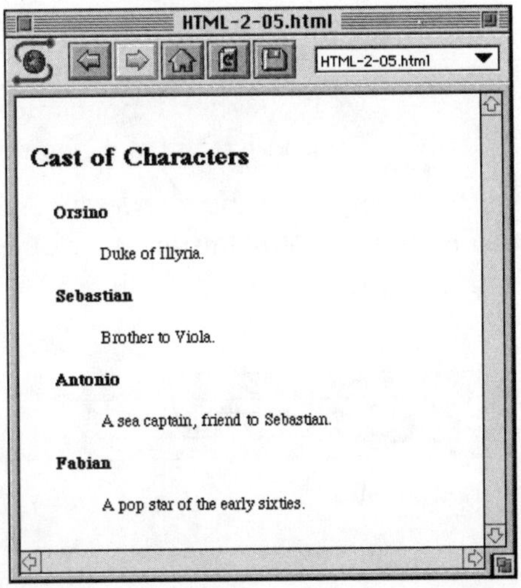

Figure 2.5: Definition list example

List tags can be specified with the COMPACT attribute <DL COMPACT>, which will reduce the amount of indenting and white space used in rendering the list.

STYLES

Style tags are an HTML level 1 feature; they may be ignored by line-mode and other minimal browsers. Graphical browsers, however, must render styled text differently than plain text. Style tags always occur in starting and ending pairs and may be nested within paragraphs and lists. Most other markup tags can occur within style tags, though the use of tags that create structure within a page—headings and lists, for example—should be avoided. Here are the most common HTML style tags:

<EM></EM>	Emphasis, usually rendered in italic or underlined to bring out the text slightly from the background text
<STRONG></STRONG>	Strong emphasis, usually rendered in boldface. Must be rendered differently than emphasis is rendered
<CITE></CITE>	Citation, for titles and references within the text, typically rendered in italic or underlined
<TT></TT>	Typewriter, a monospaced font (every character has the same width), such as Courier

Again, different browsers will render the above styles differently, and many browsers will not render each style distinct from all the others. Figure 2.6 shows the result in Mosaic of using the above text in a definition list (and adding end tags).

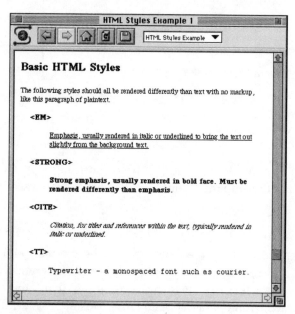

Figure 2.6: Basic HTML style tags

Bold, italic, and underline tags are defined as <B>, <I>, and <U>, respectively, for instances where exact control of the text is required—for example, when one part of the text must refer to other parts (such as "The rules specified in italics are optional."). Authors are encouraged, however, to use the more general tags to provide greater consistency between documents from different sources.

The address format tag, <ADDRESS>, is used for signatures, address elements, and other authorship information usually appearing at the top or bottom of a page. Address text is typically rendered in italic and may be indented or right justified. Unlike the tags above, the address tag implies a paragraph break before and after the text within the tag. Within the address-formatted text, use the line break tag, <BR>, instead of the paragraph tag, <P>, for greater consistency between browsers.

Another style tag that implies paragraph breaks before and after is the blockquote tag, <BLOCKQUOTE>, used for quoting segments of outside text within a page. Blockquote text may be rendered with both right and left indentation, as shown in Figure 2.7 (note the two-line address at the bottom):

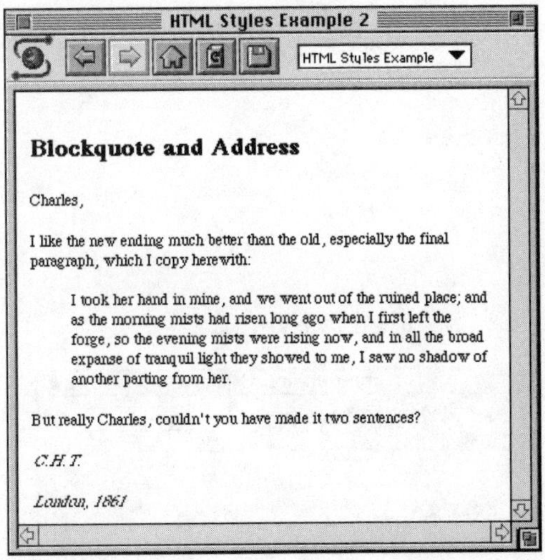

Figure 2.7: Text containing a blockquote followed by an address

One of the most important tag styles in HTML is the preformatted text tag. Any text between the starting and ending tags <PRE> and </PRE> will be left essentially as it is—well, almost, anyway. Preformatted text is rendered in a monospaced font, and all line breaks and redundant blanks are retained. This makes it ideal for text that is formatted with columns such as tables or any text where spacing must be preserved. Horizontal tabs are recognized and expanded as if there were tab stops every 8 characters across the page. However, the use of tabs is not recommended; if you can, replace any tabs in the text with space runs of appropriate length first.

Preformatted text implies a paragraph break before and after the defining tags. However, the paragraph tag, <P>, should never be used within preformatted text, nor should any tag that implies structure, such as headings and lists or address and blockquote styles. The italic, bold, and underline style tags, <I>, <B>, and <U>, and the anchor tags are the only really appropriate tags within preformatted text. Here's a simple example of preformatted text:

```
<HEAD>
<TITLE>Preformatted Text example</TITLE>
</HEAD>

<BODY>
<H2>Puzzle</H2>

<PRE>
                          |\    /
     Here's one way to    * * *
          connect all 9   |  X
     dots using only 4    * * *
       straight lines:    |/   \
                          *-*-*-
</PRE>
</BODY>
```

This will create the display shown in Figure 2.8.

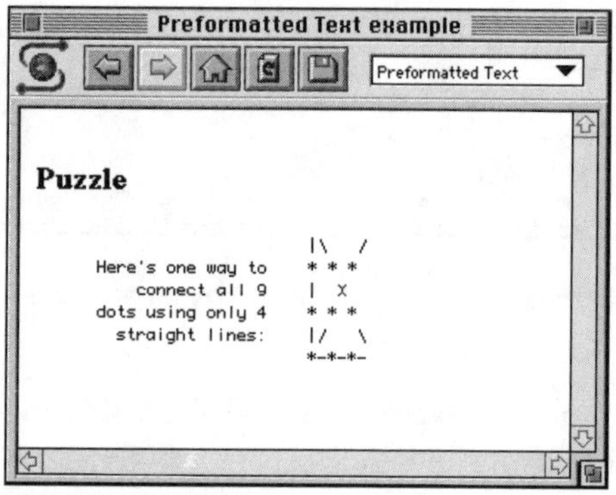

Figure 2.8: An example of preformatted text

The preformatted tag has one optional attribute, WIDTH. When specified, the WIDTH attribute tells the browser the maximum line length that can be expected within the preformatted text. With this information the browser can adjust the margins or font size to accommodate the text. Values of either 40, 80, or 132 should be used for best results. Example:

```
<PRE WIDTH=80> this is preformatted text</PRE>
```

A number of styles are defined by the HTML level 2 DTD for use in instructional manuals, computer system documentation, and user's guides:

<CODE></CODE>   Coding—for samples of computer programming, usually rendered in a monospaced font

<VAR></VAR>   Variable—in instructional text, the name of a value to be supplied by the user

<KBD></KBD>   Keyboard—a sequence of characters to be typed in, exactly, by the user

<SAMP></SAMP>   Sample—a sequence of literal characters

These next two styles were proposed for HTML level 2 and left as optional. They may be supported by some browsers:

<DFN></DFN>   Definition—the defining instance of a term, typically bold or italic

<STRIKE></STRIKE>   Strike-out text, as might appear in a legal document

The HTML plus (level 3) DTD includes these additional style tags:

    Subscript—lower the text slightly: may be rendered with a smaller font size than plain text

    Superscript—raise the text slightly; may be rendered with a smaller font size than plain text

<TR></TR>   Times Roman—a proportionally spaced serif font

<HV></HV>   Helvetica—a proportionally spaced sans-serif font

ANCHORS AND LINKS

Anchors are text strings that mark the ends of hypertext links. There are a number of attributes that can be specified with an anchor tag; two are of prime importance, the HREF and the NAME attributes. All attributes are optional;

however, an anchor needs at least a NAME or an HREF attribute to be of any use. The NAME attribute specifies that the anchor is the destination of a link. It can have an arbitrary value as long as it is unique within the document. The HREF attribute marks the attribute as the start of a hypertext link. In the simplest format, where both the start and the destination of the link are within the same document, the value of the HREF attribute is a name preceded by a pound sign (#). For example:

```
Addresses of <A HREF="#sources">additional sources</A> can be found at
the end of this chapter.
       .
       .
       .
Finally, some <A NAME="sources">more sources</A> of information.
```

In the above example, the phrase *additional sources* will be specially highlighted to indicate that the phrase is active. In Mosaic, it would be underlined and colored blue. Clicking on the phrase will cause the browser to jump to the named section somewhere else in the document. Often, the destination of a hypertext link is text that is already marked up. In these cases, the anchor should be the innermost nested tag. For example, if the destination is a heading, use

```
<H3><A NAME="sources">Sources</A></H3>
```

instead of

```
<A NAME="sources"><H3>Sources</H3></A>
```

To link to another document, a Uniform Resource Locator, or URL, is given as the value of the HREF attribute. The URL format allows the specification of almost any resource on the Internet, whether that resource is an HTML file on a Web server or some other Internet resource, such as a gopher or Usenet newsgroup. The URL has several parts, not all of which are required in order for the URL to be valid. In order of appearance, they specify the

▸ Method to be used to access the resource

▸ Name of the server providing the resource

▸ Port number to be used on the server

▸ File name of the resource

▸ Named anchor in the HTML document

The parts above are separated by various delimiters and the whole is enclosed in quotes, as follows:

```
"method://server:port/file#anchor"
```

To link to another HTML document in the same directory as the current one, only the file name is needed. The method is assumed to be *http*, which stands for *Hypertext Teleprocessing Protocol*, the Web's own creation. The following example provides a link to a file *spot_info.html*:

```
His cat is named <A HREF="spot_info.html">Spot</A>.
```

This form of link, where the source and the destination are in the same directory on the same Web server, is called a relative link. It doesn't matter how you originally linked to the server. Once you are there, everything else there is relative. Relative addressing gives your hypertext work portability since as long as the files stay together in the same logical directory, none of the relative links need to be respecified when the collection is moved from one server to another. To designate a specific address for the resolution of relative address in case a file does become physically separated from the other files in a set of hypertext pages, use the <BASE> tag in the head of the document to point to a server and directory, for example:

```
<HEAD>
<TITLE>PROJECT 2 - Table of Contents</TITLE>
<BASE HREF="http://www.myserver.com/user1/project2/">
</HEAD>
```

To link to a specific anchor in the destination, follow the file name with a pound sign and the name of the anchor, like this:

```
<A HREF="spot_info.html#habits">Spot</A>
```

Suppose the file is in a subdirectory of the directory of the current file; say, one named *pets*. A link to the file above would be written:

```
<A HREF="pets/spot_info.html">Spot</A>
```

It makes no difference how directory paths and file names are actually constructed in the operating system under which the server is running—whether backslashes separate directories, as in Windows, or square brackets are used, as in VMS—URL syntax uses slashes for all these forms. The server will be responsible for converting the request to the actual form used to reference the file.

If the file is on a different server than that of the current file, then the access method and the domain name of the server must be specified, separated by double slashes. Here's an example:

```
<A HREF= "http://ufp.enprise.mil/crew/pets/spot_info.html">
Spot</A>
```

This example assumes that the Web server, ufp.enprise.mil, is running on port 80, which is the default port for World Wide Web servers. If this is not the case—say, ufp.enprise.mil is on port 1080—then the port must be specified as follows:

```
<A HREF= "http://ufp.enprise.mil:1080/crew/pets/spot_info.html">
Spot</A>
```

As you can see, Anchors can be quite lengthy.

Other resources on the Internet besides HTML documents can be linked from an HTML document. The general philosophy is if it's out there, you can construct a URL to point to it. Specific methods exist for ftp, gopher, news, and WAIS servers, and for accessing Telnet sessions. Mosaic and other browsers will take different actions depending on the type of resource accessed. A gopher is presented as a menu structure; a file on a gopher or ftp server is downloaded to a specified directory. Here are some examples of Internet URLs:

- ftp://ftp.uu.net/doc/literary/obi/World.Factbook
- gopher://gopher.micro.umn.edu/
- Telnet://compuserve.com/
- news:alt.cows.moo

A gopher is assumed to be on the default gopher port, port 70. If the gopher uses another port, it must be specified by following the server name with a colon and the number. For the Telnet link to work, you must have access to a Telnet client.

The format for accessing Usenet newsgroups, as you can see, is different from the format for accessing other Internet resources in that it does not specify a news (NNTP) server. The server name is set somewhere else. In Mosaic, the Preferences dialog box has an entry for your default news server. Other browsers might require that the server name be specified in an environmental variable. In the future, the NNTP server name may be specified as part of the URL in a more standard fashion.

IMAGES

A picture or two will go a long way in making your Web page more attractive. The picture on your home page will give information to the reader that cannot be gleaned from the text; a simple line graph is more informative than a table of numbers. Pictures and images can also be used as decorative elements on a page, and they are especially useful in anchor elements.

To include an in-line image in your page, use the image tag, <IMG>. It's an empty tag—that is, no text is enclosed and no ending image tag is used. The image tag has four attributes:

SRC   The source attribute is mandatory. Its value is the URL of the file containing the image to be embedded. The syntax of the source attribute is the same as that of the HREF attribute used in the anchor tag.

ALIGN   The align attribute uses one of three values—TOP, MIDDLE, or BOTTOM—to define how text and graphics should be aligned.

ALT   The ALT attribute can be used to specify a text string that a nongraphical browser can display as an alternative to the in-line image.

ISMAP   The image is an interactive map. Clicking in the image will send the current cursor coordinates to a server. The image tag must be enclosed by anchor tags with an HREF attribute pointing to a script or program on the server that can map the provided coordinates to the desired Web page.

Here's an example of a page with two small, in-line images; the second image is the anchor of a link:

```
<HEAD>
<TITLE>Image Example</TITLE>
</HEAD>

<BODY>
<H1>Inline Images</H1>
<IMG SRC="Mosaic.GIF"> Mosaic is a graphical browser capable of
displaying in-line images.
<P>
Need <A HREF="http://www.ncsa.uiuc.edu/Mosaic/QuickStart.html">
<IMG SRC="More.GIF" ALT=" more " ALIGN=MIDDLE> information</A>?
</BODY>
```

Figure 2.9 shows what the reader would see in Mosaic.

In the above example, both images are decorative in that the page would function just as well without them. A line-mode browser that could not display the image would substitute the word *more*, specified as the value of the ALT attribute, as the anchor of the line. However, some line-mode browsers are capable of displaying external images through the use of a helper application. So if an image is essential to a page, you should probably add an external

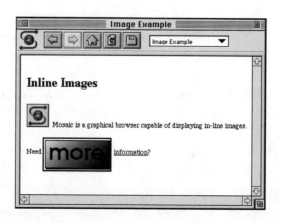

Figure 2.9: In-line images in Mosaic

link to it. The common way to do this is to make the in-line image (with an ALT attribute for line mode) a link to the external image.

To include a link to an external image in an HTML page, use an anchor with an HREF attribute in the same manner as you would for an HTML link to another hypertext page. Mosaic and other browsers recognize special file name extensions in an HREF value as follows (note that case is not significant):

HTML,HTM	Hypertext page
GIF	Image in Graphics Interchange Format
XIBM	IBM image format
PICT	Macintosh image format
JPG,JPEG	Compressed image in jpeg format
MPG,MPEG	Compressed video in mpeg format
MOV	Video in Macintosh QuickTime format
AU	Basic audio format
AIFF	Another audio format

The association between a file name extension and a helper application to display the image, video, or sound file externally is set in a Preferences dialog box in Mosaic and some other browsers. Check the user's manual for the particular browser you are using.

FORMS

Forms are an advanced feature of HTML Level 2. Only the simplest of forms will be described here. As this area of HTML is still evolving, check the on-line documentation from NCSA and CERN for a complete list of features and their use. In order to make the fullest use of forms, you will have to know the particular features of the WEB server software handling your HTML pages.

A *form* is a designated area of an HTML page made available for user input. There can be many forms on a page; however, forms cannot be nested. Each form is defined by starting and ending tags with attributes for specifying how the form's input should be processed. Below is a simple form with one input field. When the reader types a carriage return in the field, the contents of the field are sent to a script.

```
<FORM METHOD=GET ACTION="cgi-bin/search">
Please enter a keyword for searching:
<INPUT TYPE="text" NAME="key" SIZE=40>
</FORM>
```

The basic idea of a form is to present input fields to the reader for typing in text information, and radio buttons, check boxes, and pop-up menus for selecting items from option lists. Somewhere on the form is a set of action buttons, typically a *Reset* button and a *Submit* button. The Reset button, when clicked, clears the reader's input from the text fields in the form and sets all input objects back to their default values. The Submit button, when clicked, instructs the browser to take the action specified in the form's ACTION attribute (which takes a URL value) according to the method specified in the METHOD attribute. There are two action methods, METHOD=GET and METHOD=POST, that determine how the information in the form will be processed.

If the GET method is specified in the form tag, the browser constructs a *query URL* consisting of the URL of the current page containing the form, followed by a question mark, followed by the values of the form's input fields and objects. The browser sends this to a executable script or program on a server identified by the URL in the ACTION attribute. The script or program can use this information to do any number of things, such as searching and updating databases. The process ends with the server returning a new page to the reader, possibly one dynamically created by the server script. If the POST method is specified, the form's contents are sent to the server script as a data block to standard input. This is the preferred method. With both methods, anything that the script writes to standard output is sent back to the reader as a new HTML page.

This collection of interactions between browser and server is known as the Common Gateway Interface (CGI). Each server has its own set of scripts and programs needed to process information from Web pages on that server. For servers running on Unix machines, these scripts are usually written in the Perl or TCL languages and are stored in a directory with the name *cgi-bin*. For more information on the Common Gateway Interface, point your browser to NCSA's documentation at:

```
http://hoohoo.ncsa.uiuc.edu/cgi/overview.html.
```

It's possible (and sometimes convenient) to bypass the requirement of having a script on the server and process the form's contents somewhere else. This can be done by using a mailto URL as the value of the ACTION attribute as is done in the example below that generates a simple form for soliciting readers' comments. When the reader clicks the Submit button in the page illustrated in Figure 2.10, the values of input objects are sent to the e-mail address, mybox@myplace.com, as a mail message of the form:

```
name1=value1&name2=value2&...
```

where each name is the name assigned to an input object with the NAME attribute and each value is either the default value of that object or what the reader entered or chose to override the default. The disadvantage of using a mailto URL is that the interaction is one way—no new HTML page can be sent back to the reader.

```
<HEAD>
<TITLE>Form Example</TITLE>
</HEAD>

<BODY>
<H1>Comments Please</H1>
We would like to hear from you. Please use the following form to submit
any comments on our service.
<FORM METHOD=POST ACTION="mailto:mybox@myplace.com">
Please enter your name:
<INPUT TYPE="text" NAME="name" SIZE="30">
<P>
and your email address:
<INPUT TYPE="text" NAME="addr" SIZE="30">
<P>
Please select one of the following choices regarding our product:
<P>
```

```
<INPUT TYPE="radio" NAME="choice" VALUE="GREAT"> It's really great!
<INPUT TYPE="radio" NAME="choice" VALUE="GOOD"> It's pretty good
<INPUT TYPE="radio" NAME="choice" VALUE="BAD">
It's the pits!
<P>
Anything else you care to add?
use the input area below:
<TEXTAREA NAME="comment" ROWS=6 COLS=40></TEXTAREA>
<P>
Thanks for your input.
<INPUT TYPE="submit"> <INPUT TYPE="reset">
</FORM>
</BODY>
```

The reader should see a display similar to that in Figure 2.10.

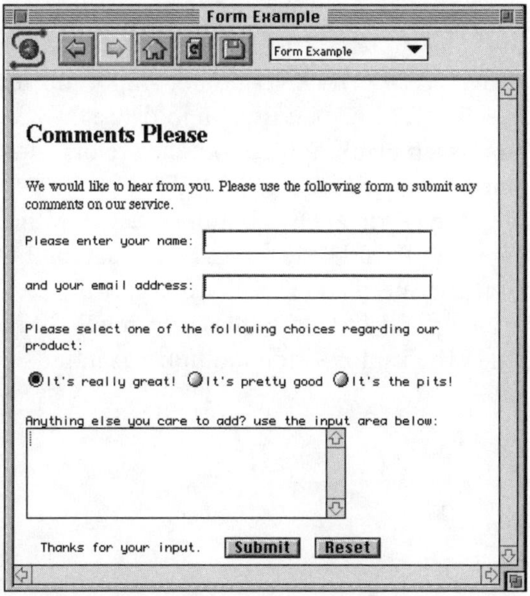

Figure 2.10: A simple forms example

The first two fields in the example request the reader's name and e-mail address with INPUT tags. The type of these input tags is *text*, indicating a single line field whose length is given by the SIZE attribute.

Following is a set of radio buttons. Radio buttons work in such a way that when one is checked, all other radio buttons with the same NAME value are automatically unchecked. Checkboxes are also supported as an input type. Checkboxes may have more than one, or none, of the choices checked.

The VALUE attribute that accompanies an input radio- or checkbox-type tag specifies the value to be sent when the form is submitted. In the above example, if the radio button to the left of the phrase *It's really great!* is the one checked, and the first two fields contain *Tom Swift* and *tswift@mars.gov,* then the mail message will contain the string

```
name=Tom+Swift&addr=tswift@mars.gov&choice=GREAT&comment=
```

As you can see, the fields are presented as *name=value* separated by ampersands (&) and with blanks replaced by plusses (+). If a field is empty, as is the case with the comment field, then the name still appears followed by the equals sign (=) and nothing else.

The TEXTAREA tag signals the beginning of a form input area of a specified number of rows and columns where the reader can enter multiple lines of text. Unlike the INPUT tag, the TEXTAREA tag is not empty; any text between it and the ending tag, </TEXTAREA>, is used to initialize the text area. In this example, the text area is left blank. You can use the preformatted text style or line-break tags to format the text for a TEXTAREA.

Finally, at the end of the form are two buttons created by the tags <INPUT TYPE="submit"> and <INPUT TYPE="reset">. The submit button signals the browser to take the action specified in the FORM tag. The reset button will, when clicked, clear all input fields within the enclosing FORM tags.

See Chapter 4, "HTML Examples," for additional examples of form usage.

Writing HTML Documents

General HTML principles

Good HTML style

Creating a home page

Converting an existing document to HTML

Chapter

3

HTML is so easy that it's tempting to jump right in and starting writing text with markup tags, checking the files with Mosaic or one of the other graphical browsers and making corrections as you go. You can put information on the World Wide Web very quickly. In a day or two, you can create an HTML hypertext work that will establish a solid presence on the Web for you or your organization. However, it's just as easy to create a sloppy hypertext work as it is to create a neat one. In this chapter you'll find a discussion of the principles of writing good World Wide Web pages, plus step-by-step walk-throughs of two kinds of Web applications—building a personal home page and converting an existing document to hypertext.

Of course, all of this is rapidly growing and changing. Perhaps the most widely observed convention found in Web documents is the inclusion of the phrase "Under Construction." You can write a home page in a few hours, but you'll never be finished with it—it will grow as you do. This is one reason observing a few principles of good design can be so important. The creation of a personal home page, in particular, is an act of creative expression in a brand new medium. It is the setting up of your booth in Cyberspace to provide information, goods, and services, and to define who you are to the Global Electronic Village.

GENERAL HTML PRINCIPLES

Another reason good design is so important with Web applications is that you have no control over the context from which people will establish links to your Web pages. Think of your Web application as a house in Cyberspace; the door is always open. Each HTML page is a room in this house. Most people will enter via your home page. A good home page takes care to properly welcome its visitors and let them know where they are and what interesting resources are to be found inside. The navigation controls of their browser will let the reader exit the way they came in; still, it's nice when the home page provides suggestions and links to other places in Cyberspace to visit.

Not everybody will enter your Web application through its home page. Some people will come in through the windows of other rooms in your Cyberspace house. There are a number of automated programs that continually explore the World Wide Web, building databases of titles, headings, and URLs as they link from one Web server to another. These are sometimes called *robots, spiders, worms,* or *web walkers.* There is a page on the Web with information on known robots at http://web.nexor.co.uk/mak/doc/robots/robots.html. You could ask the World Wide Web Worm, for example, to provide a list of all Web pages that have the word *fractal* in their title. Such links are independent of the structure the authors of those pages intended. The point is that readers will find ways you didn't anticipate to enter your hypertext work. Help these people out; at a minimum, provide a link back to your home page from every other page you put on the Web. Don't leave lost readers feeling more lost than when they entered.

Remember also that your HTML documents—the source code of your Web application—are readily available to anyone who can access the Web. Other HTML authors may copy elements of your pages and incorporate them into their Web applications. Hypertext works on the World Wide Web are living, growing structures. If you keep this in mind, with a little preparation, practice, and planning, your hypertext works can grow and evolve as smoothly as the Web does.

Probably the best preparation for writing HTML documents for the World Wide Web is reading World Wide Web HTML documents. Get a feel for what other authors have put on the Web and the approaches they've taken in organizing and formatting their work. You'll need a graphical browser to fully appreciate what others have done with HTML. You should at least have NCSA Mosaic. Other browsers may have more features than Mosaic; however, most of the documents currently on the Web have been written with Mosaic in mind. Mosaic is great software. It comes in versions for Microsoft Windows, Apple Macintosh, and Unix X/Windows, and it's free—a heck of a deal.

The home page for all three versions of Mosaic, http://www.ncsa.uiuc.edu/ SDG/Software/Mosaic, is a good place to start your study of Web pages. Another good place is NCSA's What's New page on the same server, http://www-.ncsa.uiuc.edu/SDG/Software/Mosaic/Docs/whats-new.html. This page is updated every two weeks with links to Web pages that have just been created.

It's a good sampling of what people in many different fields are doing right now on the Web with HTML.

Mosaic and most of the other graphical browsers can save any HTML document on the World Wide Web in its original form as an HTML file. It is then a simple matter to open that HTML file in a text editor to see how HTML was used to create the display seen in Mosaic's window. As practice in writing HTML documents, edit these files and change the tags. Mosaic has an Open Local… choice under its File menu that you can use to view the reedited pages to see your changes reflected in the browser's display. After looking at a number of HTML documents and playing with the elements of HTML, you should start to have an idea of what you can do with your own applications. But before you start, it's good to review a few principles that apply to computer programming in general but have special application to HTML documents on the World Wide Web.

General principle number 1: Keep it simple. Emphasize content over form. You have little control over the exact look your document will have when viewed by the various browsers readers have at their disposal, so don't waste a lot of effort trying to get something to look just right; instead, spend your time making the content—the information you want to convey to the reader— clear and compelling. If the typography of a document must be exact, consider putting a version of that document on your Web server in a format that can be downloaded by the reader—a Microsoft Word document in RTF (Rich Text Format) or an Adobe PostScript or Acrobat file, for example.

Make sure the images on your Web page are informative. A small picture of you on your home page provides readers with information that words alone cannot convey. A picture of your car, unless you've done something extraordinary with it, does not. Avoid putting up Web pages that emulate automated teller machines with large graphic buttons for links. They take too long to load and are harder to maintain. HTML provides different list structures, one of which should do to organize any set of links. As the application evolves, you'll find it a lot easier to change these list structures than you would a set of pictures. Your Web page should not look like a magazine cover, either. Readers will choose to link to your page because they are browsing related information, not because of your cool graphics. Web pages are not in competition with each other for the reader's attention.

The Internet, and the World Wide Web in particular, is growing so fast that many Internet experts are worried that bandwidth, essentially the networks' capacity to handle traffic, is starting to get scarce. So it's considered polite practice (good netiquette) to keep the amount of data you're asking others to move across their networks on your behalf to a minimum. Large graphic elements eat up bandwidth. Your PC graphics program is probably great at creating beautiful three-dimensional bar charts with gradient color fills, but you can probably provide the same information with a two-dimensional black-and-white graph. One approach commonly found on the Web is the use of a small version of a graphic, often called a thumbnail, as a link to a larger version. For example, this bit of HTML

```
Click <A HREF="Large_AE.GIF"> Albert
<IMG SRC="Small_AE.GIF" ALT="Einstein" ALIGN=MIDDLE>
</A> to see a large (90k bytes) picture of the scientist.
```

creates the Mosaic display shown in Figure 3.1.

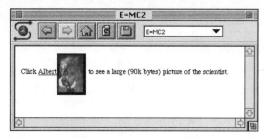

Figure 3.1: Using a thumbnail to access a larger image.

The relative URL addressing (using a partial URL to refer to the location of a file relative to the URL of the current page) used in generating Figure 3.1 requires that the two image files referenced in the HTML anchors—Large_AE.-GIF and Small_AE.GIF—be in the same directory as the Web page containing the links. The name *Albert* and the small image are together the anchor of a link to the larger image file, Large_AE.GIF. Clicking either one will fetch the larger file and pass it to a helper application to display it in a separate window as an external image. By telling readers in the text how large the image file is, you provide them with the information needed to estimate how long it will take to load. Note the use of the ALT attribute in the IMG tag to direct non-graphical browsers to display the text "Click *Albert Einstein* to see a large (90k bytes) picture of the scientist."

General principle number 2: Good work is never done. It is not until after your information is made available on the Web that you'll begin to appreciate the hypertext structure that is natural for it. You should expect to frequently update and revise any work you put on the Web. As you add to and change the information on a page, you'll have the opportunity to work with its structure, improve its looks, and replace any dead URLs—links to Web pages or servers that no longer exist. You'll also have the benefit of feedback from other people who have read your work. It's a good idea—in fact it's an accepted Web convention—to include your signature and e-mail address on your work. And don't be embarrassed to ask for comments.

A decade ago, a speaker at a computer language conference I attended formulated this principle into the following law which he named after himself. Herewith is Biddlestone's law:

> *The requirements of any system are a function of the experience gained installing that system for the user.*

One implication of this law is that whatever information you have, in whatever state it's in, you should put it up on your server and let people see it. It's better to make the information available with an explanation than to not make it available at all. It's not uncommon to come across a page on the World Wide Web (or on a gopher server) with a heading following by the phrase *Under construction* or *Work in progress*, so you should not be embarrassed to place unfinished or unverified information on your Web pages, as long as you inform your readers of this fact.

General principle number 3: Have fun :-).

The way you approach creating a hypertext work for the World Wide Web depends on what kind of information you want to serve and how much of is already in digital form. Broadly speaking, there are two approaches: top-down and bottom-up. If you are starting a work from scratch and there is little or no existing information already on line, then work from the top down. If there is already a lot of information available that needs organizing, or if there's an existing work to be converted to hypertext, then start from the bottom and work your way up. Of course, not all hypertext applications fall easily into one of these two categories. Most real-world projects are a combination of new work and existing material. This is typical of organizations that already make use of distributed information.

A third approach you might find useful is stealing. Yes, theft—if you find something you like, copy it. Edit other people's pages and replace their information with yours. You may prefer to think of this as *borrowing* ideas; if so, you should pay back the ideas with interest.

Stealing from other Web pages can be very productive. I must recommend, however, that you only copy the structure and the hypertext links, not the content from somebody else's Web page. Avoid copying anything from pages that have explicit copyright statements or that are connected to organizations with large financial and legal resources. When in doubt, ask. And give credit where it's due.

GOOD HTML STYLE

As the Web continues to grow, it becomes ever more important to write HTML that conforms to certain guidelines and styles. Right now there are about a dozen Web browsers available. A year from now I fully expect that number to triple. The major online services all have plans to provide Web browsers as part of their offerings. The new releases of the most popular operating systems, Microsoft Windows 95, Macintosh System 7.5, and OS/2 Warp have built-in Internet connectivity. This will greatly expand the potential Internet and World Wide Web user base; expect the major software publishers to respond with a flood of Web products.

So it's important to write HTML that will look good on any client, not just on Mosaic and the current generation of browsers. This section will offer some guidelines as to the do's and don'ts of writing good HTML documents that are easy to maintain and will produce presentable results on any browser. If you follow these guidelines, your document may not look its best on every browser, but it will not look ugly on any browser. Please keep in mind that none of this is written in stone. The Web, large as it is, is still in its infancy, and nobody wants to inhibit its growth—or, for that matter, yours.

It is a good idea to sign and date all documents you put on the Web so that your readers can form some impression of the authority of the document—how recent it is and how reliable the source of the information is. On a home page or any page that serves as an introduction to a hypertext work, your signature should include your full name and e-mail address so readers can send you comments on your work. You can make your name into a link to your personal home page. On less important pages of the work, your signature can just be your initials linked back to the authorship information on the home page.

You can add an external signature to a Web page by placing a link element in the heading of the page. It should be written

```
<LINK REV="made" HREF="mailto:email_address">
```

with your e-mail address appearing in place of *email_address* in the example. Place it after the title tags and before the closing </HEAD> tag. The REV (reverse relationship) indicates how this document is related to the object pointed to by the HREF URL—your e-mail address. The value *made* says that your e-mail address "made" this document. This convention is relatively new but gaining wide acceptance as a way to provide servers and browsers with your identity.

Remember that your documents are going on a *World* Wide Web, so when dating a document, use a long date format with the name of the month spelled out or abbreviated—in other words, October 1, 1994, or 1-Oct-94. Formats such as 10/1/94 can be ambiguous.

Probably the most prevalent kind of error in writing HTML is the misuse of paragraph breaks. In part this comes from working so much with one browser that you begin to accept its handling of white space as common; it also comes from the misconception that the <P> element signals an end of paragraph, rather than a paragraph break. According to the HTML specification, "<P> is used between two pieces of text which otherwise would be flowed together".

Usually this is not important. In certain contexts, however, use of extra paragraph tags should always be avoided, such as before or after any element that already implies a paragraph break. Avoid placing the <P> element either before or after headings or text marked with ADDRESS, BLOCKQUOTE, or PRE tags. You should not place paragraph tags immediately before or after a list structure or between the items of a list, either. The list item tags <LI>, <DT>, and <DD> already imply paragraph breaks. Some clarification is needed with the glossary list tags <DT> and <DD>. It is not legal HTML to have more than one <DD> tag following a defining term <DT> tag. If the definition part of the entry requires more than one paragraph of text, the use of paragraph tags to separate them is correct; the use of multiple <DD> tags per <DT> is not.

Another common source of error is not properly closing an HTML element. With character entities this means forgetting the trailing semicolon or having blanks separate the character entity from the rest of the text. It's also easy to forget that the ampersand is the escape character. Make sure you write *AT&T* and not *AT&T*. Forgetting one of the double quote marks that should enclose a URL is also a common error. Some browsers don't care if a URL is in quotes, but some do; many will have a problem if one quote mark is there and the other isn't.

With tag elements, errors can occur when the closing right angle bracket (>) is missing. Many browsers will properly render strings that contain a single right angle bracket with no matching left bracket (<) as if that character were part of the text. For example, *<This is not a tag>* will be displayed as: *<This is not a tag>*. However, it is recommended that the character entity *>* be used for the right angle bracket—*<This is not a tag>*—because if there are any other tag errors in the document, having an extra > around will only make matters worse. With nonempty markup tags, forgetting the slash (/) that begins the ending element will cause errors, as will having blanks on either side of the slash. In both cases, most (but not all) browsers will ignore the incorrect ending tag and produce the same errors as they would if you forgot the ending tag entirely. Whatever tag was in effect, its formatting would continue into the following text, possibly to the end of the page.

The nesting of tags should be done carefully. As a general rule, tags that define styles should be inside of tags that imply structure. Without enumerating all the possible combinations, here are a few guidelines:

Avoid nesting other tags inside of a heading. The big exception to this rule is anchors marking the text of the heading as the start or destination of a hypertext link. Headings should never contain any tags that imply paragraph breaks. This includes other headings, paragraph tags, horizontal rules, list structures, blockquotes, addresses, and preformatted style tags. If you want to create a multiple line heading, use the line break tag <BR>. Likewise, headings should never be enclosed in tags other than <BODY></BODY> and <FORM></FORM> and, of course, the <HTML></HTML> tags that define the document. Enclosing headings with any other tags doesn't make sense, and the results are unpredictable.

The use of style tags to change the rendering of a heading should be avoided except when applied to a small part of the heading text, for example:

```
<H3>Some <STRONG>Important</STRONG> phone numbers<H3>.
```

Image tags can be used inside of a heading to provide a small graphic counterpart to the heading text. Having the image inside the heading tags is necessary for the browser to recognize the ALIGN attribute and place the image properly with respect to the heading text.

Anchors should be the innermost items of a set of nested tags. For example:

```
<H3>William Shakespeare</H3>
An English playwright ....etc., etc.,
<UL>
<LI><CITE><A HREF="...">Macbeth</A></CITE>
<LI>...
</UL>
```

One last point with regard to tags is that you should avoid using any obsolete tags; they can creep into your work if you copy parts of it from other pages on the Web. These elements include <PLAINTEXT></PLAINTEXT>, <XMP></XMP>, <LISTING></LISTING>, <HPx></HPx>, and <COMMENT></COMMENT>. The first three should be replaced with the preformatted tags <PRE></PRE>; <HP></HP> (highlighted phrase) should be replaced with appropriate style tags; and <COMMENT></COMMENT> should be replaced with SGML comments which are enclosed by the strings <!-- and -->.

URLs can be a source of errors. A URL error won't affect the rendering of the page in a browser's display, but a badly composed URL may be incorrectly interpreted by some browsers. Relative URLs, which are used in the next two sections of this chapter, have strong advantages—they're shorter and they make a collection of documents more portable. However, relative URLs should be used with care since the URL does not contain all the information necessary to construct the link. The missing server and path information is taken by the browser from the URL of the document that contains the link. Unfortunately, not all browsers do this exactly the same way. What is always safe is a relative reference to a file in the same directory as the current page. Files in a subdirectory can usually be referenced by using slash—a forward slash (/), not the backslash (\) used in DOS path names—as in:

```
our clerk, <A HREF="staff/Cratchet.html">Bob Cratchet</A>
```

You can also refer to the same file above by using a dot to refer to the current directory:

```
our clerk, <A HREF="./staff/Cratchet.html">Bob Cratchet</A>
```

You can refer to the parent directory by using two dots (..). However, this may not work with all browsers and servers. To be absolutely safe, any files that are not in the same directory as the current page should be referenced by their full path and file names.

Be careful with the use of the *file* URL method. What this is supposed to do is reference the file on the local host of whoever is browsing the document. This might be a file on your hard disk or it might be a file on your Internet server provider's computer. It is not supposed to be a file on the Web server pointed to by the current URL. Unfortunately, some early browsers treat *file* as synonymous with *ftp*. Unless you know what you are doing, avoid using this URL method.

These are only some of the more common sources of error. Developing a good HTML style is a matter of practice, studying the work of others, and finally, good common sense.

CREATING A HOME PAGE

A home page is the one hypertext document within a work that is intended as the primary starting point of the work. This is where the work is introduced and placed in the larger context in which it's contained. This definition has to be a bit abstract as it depends partially on the reader's point of view. The World Wide Web can be viewed as a single hypertext work, albeit one with many authors. The default home page for the Web is at CERN, the European Center for High Energy Physics Research. The URL is

```
http://info.cern.ch/hypertext/WWW/TheProject.html
```

Your personal home page is the starting point for all of your hypertext works. Since it will be created from scratch, I recommend using a top-down approach, starting with a simple outline like this:

I. Your Name
   1. A welcome message
   2. Information about you
   3. A statement of your goals
   4. Current activities/announcements
   5. Related information
   6. Signature, address, time stamps

You needn't follow the above outline exactly, but this is the information readers generally expect to see on a personal home page.

Before you begin editing the HTML files you need somewhere to put them. Create a new directory for these files. A subdirectory of the one that contains Mosaic or your favorite browser is a good location as it will keep your path names short. Figure 3.3 refers to this directory as *WebSpace*; you can name your directory anything you want. Into this new directory place a text file containing an HTML template. Give this file an obvious file name such as *template.html*. If your operating system supports stationary or read-only documents, you should save this template as such to prevent overwriting it accidentally. Make sure you also save it as a plain text file instead of saving in your word processor's normal format. Next start with a copy of the template file and fill in the TITLE and BODY sections based on the outline above, like so:

```
<HTML>
<HEAD>
<TITLE>Johannes Kepler's Home Page</TITLE>
</HEAD>

<BODY>
<H1>Johannes Kepler</H1>
<STRONG>Welcome to my Home Page!</STRONG>
<HR>
<H2>Who am I</H2>
<H2>What is this Document</H2>
<H2>Current Projects</H2>
<H2>Related Information</H2>
<HR>
<ADDRESS>
```

```
Johannes Kepler &lt;kepler@nasa.gov&gt;
</ADDRESS>
Created: September 26, 1994,
Updated: September 27, 1994
</BODY>
</HTML>
```

and save it in WebSpace directory as homepage.html. All HTML documents should have filenames that end with the extension *.html* unless the files reside on a DOS system, in which case they should have the extension *.htm*. If you now load this file into Mosaic, you'll get the display shown in Figure 3.2.

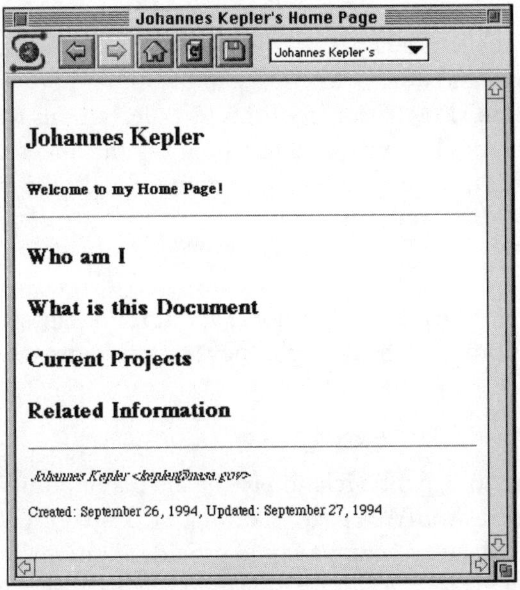

Figure 3.2: Johannes Kepler's home page—first draft

From here on, it's just a matter of filling in paragraphs of narrative text under each heading with perhaps some subheadings and maybe a picture of yourself. At this stage, don't worry about the hypertext structure; that will evolve as you develop the page from the top downward. If you find that under some heading you are just listing items, then use one of the HTML list structures. A common feature of many home pages is a list of links to the author's favorite Internet sites. Put such lists under the *Related Information* heading.

Now read what you've written. Did you mention the World Wide Web? If you did, then make that reference into a link to the World Wide Web's home page at CERN:

```
<A HREF="http://info.cern.ch/hypertext/WWW/TheProject.html">
World Wide Web</A>
```

Likewise for any organizations that you refer to in the text that have home pages on the Web.

Do you have a copy of your resumé on line? If you do, then create a plain text version of that file and save it in the WebSpace directory as *resume.txt*. The *.txt* extension (and the lack of <HTML></HTML> tags) tells browsers not to interpret the file as a hypertext document—in other words, to respect the carriage returns and other white space in the file and present it as is. Later on you can create an HTML version of this text file, but this will do for now. Your file structure should now look something like the directory listing (slightly simplified) in Figure 3.3. In the section that tells the reader who you are, make a link to the text file, like this:

```
...can see my <A HREF="resume.txt">resume</A>, if you wish.
```

Try to incorporate the text that anchors hypertext links into the natural flow of the paragraph's prose, as the example above does and not refer to the anchor text explicitly, as in:

```
Click <A HREF="resume.txt">here</A> to see my resume.
```

The word *here* has no semantic relation to the file that it points to. That is, if a program should scan your Web page recording each anchor URL and its associated anchor text, the word *resume* would provide additional information about the file it points to; the word *here* would not. Besides, you can pretty well assume that the readers know what is and what is not a link by the time they get to your page.

The entire home page should not be more than a few screens. If any section starts getting more than a few paragraphs long, it's time to create a new page and link to it from your home page. For example, suppose under the heading *Who am I* you list your favorite activity, astronomy. In the same manner that you created your home page, create a astronomy page containing a description of your equipment, your favorite planets, and perhaps, a link to the Usenet newsgroup news:sci.astro. Save the astronomy page in the WebSpace directory and on your home page, making the word "astronomy" into a link, like so:

```
blah, blah, blah, favorite activity:
<A HREF="astronomy.html">astronomy</A>.
```

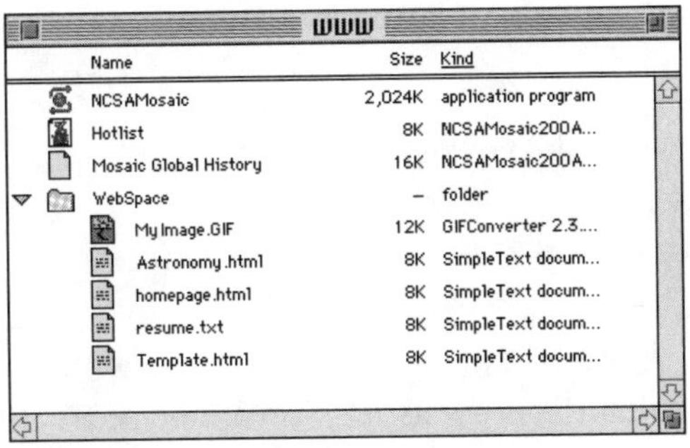

Figure 3.3: Directory structure of a simple home page

By keeping all the files in the same directory as your home page, all the links can be specified relatively with simple file names. When you copy these documents to a directory on a Web server, these links will still be valid. This way, you maintain a local working copy of your Web application that mirrors what you have available on the Web.

The final touch is to add your picture to your home page. There are many ways to get a picture onto your computer—scanner, digital camera, Photo CD—and the image file formats differ from one operating system to another. However you got your picture onto your computer and whatever file format it is in, it must be converted into one of two image file formats, GIF or JPEG, before you put it up in your WebSpace as a part of your home page.

Graphic Interchange Format (GIF) is the older and more commonly found format. It was invented by Compuserve and is widely used on the Internet and BBSs for downloadable images. It is the preferred format for inline images. JPEG, a standard developed by the Joint Photographic Equipment Group, is newer and not yet supported by many browsers. It incorporates data compression so that an image file in JPEG format can be considerably smaller than the same image in GIF format. There are many utilities programs, both shareware and freeware, for converting files from one image format to another.

When an image is expanded in a Web page, it is treated as if it were a character of text. If the image follows an explicit or implied paragraph break, it will be positioned at the left margin of the page. If the image begins with or is embedded in a line of text, that text will be aligned with the top, middle, or bottom of the image according to the value of the ALIGN attribute. No space is inserted either before or after the image to separate it from the text it is embedded in; you must explicitly provide that space, if you want it there.

It's quite permissible to place an image in a heading, for example:

```
<H2><IMG SRC="kepler.gif" ALIGN=MIDDLE> Johannes Kepler</H2>
```

or to use an image as the anchor of a link, as in

```
<A HREF="kepler.html">
<IMG SRC="kepler.gif" ALT="Johannes Kepler" ALIGN=BOTTOM>
</A>
```

Note the use of the ALT attribute; without it, readers with nongraphical browsers wouldn't know what the link was. All they would see is [IMAGE].

Unfortunately, there's no provision in HTML level 2 for wrapping text around an image. One thing that you can do, however, is make a transparent GIF image. The GIF format allows one color on the image pallet to be transparent so that when the image is placed on top of the background color of the display page, the background shows through whatever pixels have that color. Transparent GIFs are especially useful for placing images on a page so that they appear without a border, such as lettering in a fancy or colored typeface. See Chapter 4, Figure 4.7, for a home page with a transparent GIF image.

CONVERTING AN EXISTING DOCUMENT TO HTML

In contrast to creating a home page, converting an existing document to hypertext is best approached from the bottom up. Suppose you have a user's guide for some aspect of your business. It could even be a guide to using the Internet. We will assume that the document is *rich text*, a general term for any document that's more than a simple text file. A rich-text document uses type styles and sizes, margins, and line spacing. The ability to create rich-text documents is what distinguishes word processing programs, such as Microsoft Word, WordPerfect, and MacWrite, from text editors. SGML languages such as HTML provide machine-independent methods for adding rich-text information to a plain text document. Hypertext documents on World Wide Web servers are text files, so first you have to create a plain text version of the guide before you build it back up to rich text with HTML elements.

Working from the bottom up, you'll create a series of versions, each a refinement of the previous one. When the conversion of the guide is completed, you'll have a full hypertext version consisting of linked files, a single file version suitable for printing, a text-only version for readers with nongraphical browsers, and the original version in a stuffed and encoded form for downloading via ftp. On top of all this, you can create a home page for the guide that describes the work and has links to the various versions as well as authorship and status information and links to related works.

Let's assume that our user's guide is written and maintained in Microsoft Word. The first thing to do is create a new directory for the project—let's call it *Guide.* It can be a subdirectory of WebSpace or a sibling, whatever is appropriate to the relation of this work to your other hypertext works. Make working copies of the file (don't work on the original), one in Microsoft Word's normal format and one in text-only format, and put them in the Guide directory. Give the latter a file name ending in the extension *.txt.* This file is what you will point out to readers with line-mode browsers. Later you may want to edit this text-only version and put in notations where the figures and illustrations were.

Go back to the working copy in normal format. It will be the base from which the other versions are created. You can create the ftp version from this file by stuffing and encoding it. *Stuffing* compacts the file by removing excess space, *encoding* creates a 7-bit portable version of the file, allowing it to be moved and stored as a text file on any kind of operating system. Place the new file in the Guide directory.

Before you can add any markup tags to the working copy of the file you must replace the special characters that are needed for HTML markup with appropriate character entities. First do a global replace of the ampersand with string *&* This will ensure that the final HTML document will be free of any unintended character entities. Next, replace all occurrences of the left angle bracket (<) and right angle bracket (>) with the strings *<* and *>,* respectively, to ensure that the only markup tags in the document are the ones you intended to be there. Then try to find and replace any of the special characters in the text from the ISO Latin-1 character set (such as å or ç), curly quotes, and symbols.

Horizontal tabs present a problem as they are not interpreted uniformly by all browsers, although most browsers will ignore them completely except in pre-formatted text. It's generally a good idea to get rid of as many tabs as possible by replacing them with an appropriate number of blanks. Delete any tabs that are used only for paragraph indentation and enclose any tables or other non-paragraph text with the preformatted style markup tags <PRE> and </PRE> to preserve their line breaks and spacing. Later on, you can go back and replace some of the preformatted sections with other HTML structures.

Note: The specification for HTML+ includes a TABLE markup. At the time of this writing, that specification is not complete and I can't recommend using it. This may change by the time you read this.

If there are figures and illustrations in the file (figures have captions, illustrations do not), they will have to be copied to individual files and removed from the text. Use a file-naming convention that preserves the image's location—for example, GUIDE03-F04.PICT—for the fourth figure in Chapter 3 of the guide. The leading zeros in the file name will insure proper sorting in a directory listing if you have more than nine items. The .PICT extension used here indicates that this file is in the Macintosh PICT format. These image files now have to be encoded into the GIF format. As you remove each figure and illustration, leave an in-line image tag in its place with an ALT attribute describing it—for example

```
<IMG SRC="GUIDE03-F04.GIF" ALT="Fig. 3-4. A typical Gopher menu">
```

As with any other computer project, save frequently and make backups.

Remove any headers and footers from the guide, since you have no control over how many lines a browser will display per page or screen and page numbering is not important in hypertext works. At the beginning of the file create an HTML head section with the main title enclosed in title tags, followed by the starting tag for the body section, followed by the main title again as a level 1 heading. Place the matching end tags at the end of the file. It should look something like this:

```
<HTML>
<HEAD>
<TITLE>Internet Guide</TITLE>
</HEAD>
<!-- Guide.html, a hypertext guide to the Internet -->
<!-- Converted from MS Word file: INT_GUIDE        -->
<!-- J. Kepler, September 29, 1994.                -->
<BODY>
<H1>Internet Guide</H1>
...
{ rest of the file }
...
</BODY>
</HTML>
```

Save this file as a text-only file. Give it a file name with .*html* as the extension— Guide.html will do. Next, starting from the beginning of the file, work your way through, placing line breaks (<BR>) and paragraph (<P>) tags where needed and enclosing headings in heading tags. Use heading level 2 for the major divisions of the guide, level 3 for the next level, and so on. As you go through the file, enclose any styled text with appropriate tags—<STRONG></STRONG> for boldface text, <EM></EM>for underlined text, <CITE></CITE> for text in italics, and so forth. Try to avoid using the explicit style tags <B></B>, <U></U>, and <I></I> unless that style is explicitly referrred to within the text. Look for places in the text where HTML lists can be used to structure information you previously marked as preformatted text. When you've completed this pass, the first draft of the HTML version of the guide is finished. Save this file. Your directory should now look something like Figure 3.4:

Name	Size	Kind
NCSAMosaic	2,024K	application program
Hotlist	8K	NCSAMosaic200A...
Mosaic Global History	16K	NCSAMosaic200A...
WebSpace	–	folder
My Image.GIF	12K	GIFConverter 2.3....
Astronomy.html	8K	SimpleText docum...
homepage.html	8K	SimpleText docum...
resume.txt	8K	SimpleText docum...
Template.html	8K	SimpleText docum...
Guide	–	folder
Guide.hqx	92K	document
Guide03-F04.GIF	12K	GIFConverter 2.3....
Guide.html	20K	Microsoft Word do...
Guide.txt	20K	Microsoft Word do...
INT_GUIDE	220K	Microsoft Word do...

Figure 3.4: Directory listing with "Guide" files

It's time to load your work into Mosaic and see what it looks like. Print it out and show it around. You may at this point want to work with an HTML editor or a text editor with HTML extensions; See Appendix C for some of the software now available.

The next step is to go through the file adding anchors and links. Make the text of each of the major headings a named anchor. Use the heading's index from the table of contents as the name, for example:

```
<H3><A NAME="G32">3.2 Gopher</A></H3>
```

In the table of contents, create a link to each of these headings:

```
<LI><A HREF="#G32">3.2 Gopher</A>
```

Do the same with any footnotes in the work. If there are references to other documents on your network or references to resources on the Internet, create links to them as well. If you're not sure about the URL, make a guess. An incorrect URL will not crash the system; you can repair these bad links when you have the correct information.

When you are finished with this process you'll have the long hypertext version of the guide. This version will be more suitable for printing than your final version will be, but will still be suitable for online browsing (although it may take some time to load over a slow line). Take some time to clean up and test this version, using different browsers if possible. If the original guide had a glossary, an index, or a quick reference section, now is the time to decide how to implement these features in hypertext.

When the long version is fairly stable, decide how to break it up into separate files. Having a hypertext work in a series of linked files has several advantages. The individual files are faster to load and the reader can have more than one section of the work displayed at the same time. Ideally, no single part of the guide should be more than a dozen screens worth of information. The exception to this is very long list structures, which should go into separate files for easier maintenance. The table of contents will go into the guide's home page. If a section of the guide is long and has many subsections, consider creating a mini–home page for that section with its own, linked mini–table of contents.

Each file will have to begin and end with the HTML tags defining the head and body of the page. Copy the title of the work as a whole and make it a level 1 heading as the very first element of the page body of each file so your readers know what they're reading. Put a horizontal rule under the level 1 heading and you have a page header. Here is what the beginning of the Chapter 3 page might look like:

```
<HTML>
<HEAD>
<TITLE>Internet Guide, Chap. 3</TITLE>
</HEAD>
<!-- Guide03.html, Chapter 3 of Internet Guide    -->
<!-- Converted from MS Word file: INT_GUIDE        -->
<!-- J. Kepler, September 29, 1994.                -->
<BODY>
<H1>Internet Guide</H1>
<HR>
<H2><A NAME="G30">Chapter 3 - Clients</A></H2>
A nice introductory paragraph should go here.
<H3>Contents</H3>
<MENU COMPACT>
<LI><A HREF="#G31">ftp</A>
<LI><A HREF="#G32">Gopher</A>
<LI><A HREF="#G33">...</A>
</MENU>
<H3><A NAME="G31">3.1 ftp</A></H3>
...
```

Any links to anchors that are now in different files must be updated to include the file name of the destination. Links in other files to anchors in this file, Guide03.html, will also have to be updated. The home page for the entire guide will contain the table of contents, the introduction, the guide's authorship information (make your name a link to your personal home page) and links to related works.

A nice touch is to add a set of navigation buttons to the bottom of each page in the guide. This next bit of HTML, at the end of the file for Chapter 3, creates a set of four text buttons that link to other files of the guide. The last link, [CONTENTS], goes to an anchor named *ToC* on the guide's home page, the file GuideHome.html. You can also use small icons for these buttons, but each icon will have to be in a separate file. Following the buttons is a link back to the authorship information on the guide's home page.

```
<HR>
<A HREF="GuideHome.html">[TOP]</A>
<A HREF="Guide02.html">[PREVIOUS]</A>
<A HREF="Guide04.html">[NEXT]</A>
<A HREF="GuideHome.html#ToC">[CONTENTS]</A>
<ADDRESS>
<A HREF="Guide.Home#author">JK</A>
</ADDRESS>
</BODY>
</HTML>
```

Figure 3.5 shows what Chapter 3 page (minus a lot of the middle) looks like in Mosaic.

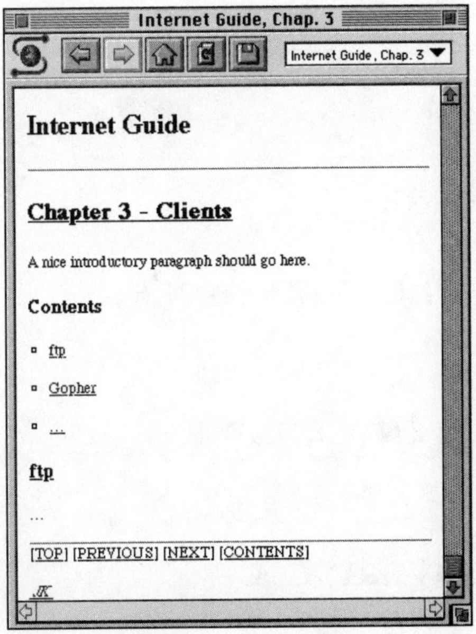

Figure 3.5: Home page for a chapter

HTML Examples

EXAMPLE 1—A PERSONAL HOME PAGE

EXAMPLE 2—A VIEWER INTEREST SURVEY

EXAMPLE 3—A SMALL ORGANIZATION'S HOME PAGE

EXAMPLE 4—A BROCHURE

EXAMPLE 5—A LARGE ORGANIZATION'S HOME PAGE

EXAMPLE 6—A PAGE OF INTERNET RESOURCES

EXAMPLE 7—A PAGE COVERING A SUBJECT FIELD

EXAMPLE 8—ANOTHER HOME PAGE

Chapter

4

I n this chapter I've collected a number of examples of World Wide Web pages. Each example includes a presentation and discussion of the HTML source of the example Web page followed by its reproduction. The examples were chosen with variety in mind to let you know what you can do with HTML and your information. Not all of the pages represent the best HTML use. That's perfectly all right. This is the work of busy people, motivated by the desire to make their information public with tools that are still evolving. I'll point out instances of poor (in my opinion) HTML use here and there, and I hope the authors won't think I'm being judgmental. I've written a zillion lines of code over the years and would hate to have anyone judge my work on such a small sample.

These examples pages are still evolving. What are presented here are snapshots of pages at that particular point in time when I found them. I'm providing the URLs of the example pages with no guarantee that they will continue to be valid, and certainly no guarantee that the pages seen on the Web at those addresses will be the same as those presented here. If they are, hopefully you'll see improvements.

Note: For each of the examples presented in this chapter, I've shown printed output of the Web page rather than the screen display. This allows for better resolution and a lot of saved work since, for most of the examples, I would have had to splice together several screens. The printouts, saved as PostScript files, have the same look as the screens without the work of scrolling.

EXAMPLE 1—A PERSONAL HOME PAGE

This first example is the home page of Gary Welz at http://found.cs.nyu.edu/found.a/CAT/misc/welz/. As you can see from the information on the page, Gary is very active in World Wide Web affairs. I like this page because it has one of the best collection of Web links I've found. This is a good home page; note how the anchors are part of the natural flow of prose in the paragraphs. Not one "click here" is used. My only criticism is that the list of links to his favorite WWW sites is so strong that it tends to overpower the paragraphs containing Gary's credentials and the information on his current projects.

Gary's home page is also a good illustration of how forgiving browsers can be. There are no <HEAD></HEAD> and <BODY></BODY> tags and the page just begins with the title. Note also that none of the HREFs are in quotes and blanks are freely used around equal signs. Even though mistakes like these will be ignored by most browsers, they should be corrected. Browsers are supposed to be forgiving; HTML authors (human and otherwise) should not be. Sticking to "canonical" HTML ensures that your pages and links function for all browsers and other programs that read your pages.

The page begins with a black-and-white image of Gary, which loads quickly on a slow link (good idea). The image is embedded in the level 1 heading and is aligned with the rest of the heading text level with the middle of the image.

```
<TITLE>Gary Welz's Home Page</TITLE>

<H1><IMG ALIGN = middle SRC = gary2.gif> Gary Welz's Home Page</H1>
<P>
This is a home page for the collection of WWW documents being created and
collected by Gary Welz, who will be teaching a seminar at the NYU Center for
Digital Multimedia on Mosaic, the World Wide Web and authoring in HTML.
<P>
<A HREF= HTMLDemo1.html>A Mosaic/HTML Demo Document</A>
that I use in HTML classes.
<P>
<A HREF= http://www.cuny.edu/~gary/arshtml/lanlarstitle.html>
The Art of Renaissance Science</A>, an HTML article authored by CUNY Historian of
Science, Joseph W. Dauben.  It is a prototype of a hypermedia journal article.
<P>
A talk I gave last summer at the 7th Conference and General Assembly of the
International Federation of Science Editors entitled:
<A HREF=internettv.html>
Television on the Internet - Scientific Publishing in a New Medium</A>. It also
contains abbreviated presentations by hardware and software vendors for Sun, Apple
and Macromedia products.
<P>
```

EXAMPLE 1—A PERSONAL HOME PAGE **59**

```
A hypermedia version of an article of mine entitled
<A HREF=interact.html>
Hypermedia, Multimedia and Television on the Internet:  Some of the best tools in
life are free</A>, that appeared in the July 1994 issue of <I>Interactions</I>, a
publication of the Association for Computing Machinery.
<P>
The  abstract of a talk I gave at the 2nd International WWW conference in Chicago
on October 18, 1994:
<A HREF= mediabusiness.html>
Abstract of: The Media Business on the WWW</A> and a draft of the paper itself: <A
HREF=WelzWWWconf2.html>The Media Business on the WWW</A>
<P>
A link to the "Call for Participation" and "Viewer Interest Survey" of the <A
HREF=http://www.service.com/stv/setncall.html>
Science and Engineering Television Network,Inc.</A> a not-for-profit corporation
that I founded with the support of the Alfred P. Sloan Foundation, the Association
for Computing Machinery, the American Physical Society,the IEEE, the American
Mathematical Society and other organizations.
<P>
My <A HREF=welzresume.html>hypertext resume</A>.
<P>
```

The rest of Gary's home page consists of links to his favorite WWW sites. These links are organized as unordered lists under several level 3 and level 4 headings. Gary places paragraph marks, <P>, after some of the lists and before the next heading. This should be avoided since there are already implied paragraph breaks there. All of the links are to HTML pages on other Web sites except for the reference to the Sumex-Aim ftp site at Stanford University.

```
<H2>A few of my favorite WWW sites:</H2>

<H3>Internet Organizations and Resources</H3>
<UL>
<LI>
<A HREF=http://www.ncsa.uiuc.edu/SDG/Software/Mosaic/MetaIndex.html>
Internet Resources Meta-Index</A>
<LI><A HREF=http://www.ncsa.uiuc.edu/SDG/Software/Mosaic/StartingPoints/NetworkStar
tingPoints.html>Network Starting Points</A>
<LI><A HREF=http://info.cern.ch/hypertext/DataSources/WWW/Servers.html>
The Web Servers Directory</A>
<LI><A HREF=http://white.nosc.mil/info.html>
The Planet Earth home page</A>
<LI><A HREF=http://info.isoc.org/home.html>The Internet Society</A>
<LI><A HREF=ftp://sumex-aim.stanford.edu/>The sumex-aim ftp site</A>
</UL>
<P>
```

```
<H3>Scientific Organizations, Institutions and Resources</H3>
<UL>
<LI><A HREF=http://aps.org>The American Phyical Society</A>
<LI><A HREF=http://aip.org>The American Institute of Phyics</A>
<LI><A HREF=http://www.acm.org/>
The Association for Computing Machinery</A>
<LI><A HREF=http://www.geom.umn.edu>
The Geometry Center at the University of Minnesota</A>
<LI><A HREF=http://stsci.edu/top.html>The Space Telescope Institute</A>
<LI><A HREF=http://bang.lanl.gov/video>
Los Alamos National Laboratory Video Server</A>
<LI><A HREF=http://www.lcs.mit.edu/>MIT Lab for Computer Science</A>
<LI><A HREF=http://www.cshl.org/>Cold Spring Harbor Lab</A>
<LI><A HREF=http://cbl.leeds.ac.uk/nikos/tex2html/doc/latex2html/
latex2html.html>A source for a Latex to HTML Translator</A>
</UL>
<P>


<H3>Electronic Media:</H3>
<H4>"Magazines"</H4>
<UL>
<LI><A HREF=http://nearnet.gnn.com/gnn/gnn.html>
Global Network Navigator</A>
<LI><A HREF=http://figment.fastman.com/vweb/html/vidmain.html>
VideoWebalog</A>
<LI><A HREF=http://www.wired.com>Wired Magazine</A>
<LI><A HREF=http://jefferson.village.virginia.edu/pmc/>
Postmodern Culture</A>
</UL>


<H4>Audio/Video/Multimedia</H4>
<UL>
<LI><A HREF=http://www.eeb.ele.tue.nl/mpeg/index.html>
The MPEG Movie Archive</A>
<LI><A HREF=http://www.acm.uiuc.edu/rml/>Rob's New Multimedia Lab</A>
<LI><A HREF=http://www.cs.ucl.ac.uk/mice/mice.html>
MICE or Multimedia Integrated Conferencing for Europe</A>
<LI><A HREF=http://www.town.hall.org/>Internet Multicasting Service</A>
<LI><A HREF=http://juggler.lanl.gov/itr.html>Internet Talk Radio</A>
<LI><A HREF=http://www.mtv.com>The MTV.com server run by Adam Curry</A>
</UL>
<P>
```

Just a note on the last item above. The MTV.com server run by Adam Curry is no longer at www.mtv.com. Accessing this site will get you a disclaimer. Adam, once an MTV VJ, registered the domain name *mtv.com* and set up a server for

Example 1—A personal home page **61**

the MTV site on his own initiative and with his own funds, apparently with the blessing (or at least benign neglect) of MTV. After the appearance of articles in the *New York Times* and the *Wall Street Journal* on the importance of Internet domain-name ownership, MTV threatened to sue Adam over the right to the name. Adam Curry's new Web site is http://metaverse.com/. Check it out—there are lots of links to music industry sites and great graphics.

```
<H3>Internet Business Info</H3>
<UL>
<LI><A HREF=http://www.tig.com/IBC/NetStats/Names.html>
IBC: Venture Capital Firms on the Net</A>
<LI><A HREF=http://ibd.ar.com/>Internet Business Directory</A>
<LI><A HREF=http://ginko.cecer.army.mil:8000/hypernews/www-leasing.html>
WWW Space Leasing Info</A>
</UL>
<P>


<H3>Electronic Marketing:</H3>
<UL>
<LI><A HREF=http://www.mecklerweb.com>MecklerWeb</A>
<LI><A HREF=http://www.branch.com/>Branch</A>
<LI><A HREF=http:///cybersight.com/cgi-bin/imi/s?main.gmml>
Internet Marketing, Inc.</A>
<LI><A HREF=http://apollo.co.uk>Apollo Advertising</A>
<LI><A HREF=http://www.service.com>Internet Distribution Service</A>
<LI><A HREF=http://marketplace.com/>Marketplace.Com</A>
<LI><A HREF=http://www.ip.net/>Internet Presence and Publishing</A>
<LI><A HREF=http://www.nets.com/>Studio X</A>
<LI><A HREF=http://www.commerce.net/>Commerce Net</A>
<LI><A HREF=http://shop.internet.net/>Internet Shopping Network</A>
<LI><A HREF=http://www.img.om.com/img/default.html>Ogilvy and Mather</A>
<LI><A HREF=http://netmarket.com/>Net Market Company</A>
<LI><A HREF=http://awa.com>Downtown Anywhere</A>
</UL>
<P>


<H3>Just Cool Sites:</H3>
<UL>
<LI><A HREF=http://sailfish.peregrine.com/WebWorld/welcome.html>
WebWorld</A>
<LI><A HREF=http://cybersight.com/cgi-bin/imi/s?main.gmml>Cybersight</A>
<LI><A HREF=http://www.service.com/stv/>Science Television</A>
</UL>
<P>


<I>Gary Welz,</I> gary@setn.org<P>
```

Figure 4.1 shows how the Web page generated by this HTML code will look when displayed and printed using NCSA Mosaic.

Gary Welz's Home Page

This is a home page for the collection of WWW documents being created and collected by Gary Welz, who will be teaching a seminar at the NYU Center for Digital Multimedia on Mosaic, the World Wide Web and authoring in HTML.

A Mosaic/HTML Demo Document that I use in HTML classes.

The Art of Renaissance Science, an HTML article authored by CUNY Historian of Science, Joseph W. Dauben. It is a prototype of a hypermedia journal article.

A talk I gave last summer at the 7th Conference and General Assembly of the International Federation of Science Editors entitled: Television on the Internet - Scientific Publishing in a New Medium. It also contains abbreviated presentations by hardware and software vendors for Sun, Apple and Macromedia products.

A hypermedia version of an article of mine entitled Hypermedia, Multimedia and Television on the Internet: Some of the best tools in life are free, that appeared in the July 1994 issue of *Interactions*, a publication of the Association for Computing Machinery.

The abstract of a talk I gave at the 2nd International WWW conference in Chicago on October 18, 1994: Abstract of: The Media Business on the WWW and a draft of the paper itself: The Media Business on the WWW

A link to the "Call for Participation" and "Viewer Interest Survey" of the Science and Engineering Television Network,Inc. a not-for-profit corporation that I founded with the support of the Alfred P. Sloan Foundation, the Association for Computing Machinery, the American Physical Society,the IEEE, the American Mathematical Society and other organizations.

My hypertext resume.

A few of my favorite WWW sites:

Internet Organizations and Resources

- Internet Resources Meta-Index

Figure 4.1: Gary Welz's home page

EXAMPLE 1—A PERSONAL HOME PAGE **63**

- Network Starting Points
- The Web Servers Directory
- The Planet Earth home page
- The Internet Society
- The sumex-aim ftp site

Scientific Organizations, Institutions and Resources

- The American Phyical Society
- The American Institute of Phyics
- The Association for Computing Machinery
- The Geometry Center at the University of Minnesota
- The Space Telescope Institute
- Los Alamos National Laboratory Video Server
- MIT Lab for Computer Science
- Cold Spring Harbor Lab
- A source for a Latex to HTML Translator

Electronic Media:

"Magazines"

- Global Network Navigator
- VideoWebalog
- Wired Magazine
- Postmodern Culture

Audio/Video/Multimedia

- The MPEG Movie Archive
- Rob's New Multimedia Lab
- MICE or Multimedia Integrated Conferencing for Europe
- Internet Multicasting Service
- Internet Talk Radio
- The MTV.com server run by Adam Curry

Internet Business Info

- IBC: Venture Capital Firms on the Net
- Internet Business Directory
- WWW Space Leasing Info

Electronic Marketing:

- MecklerWeb
- Branch
- Internet Marketing, Inc.
- Apollo Advertising
- Internet Distribution Service
- Marketplace.Com
- Internet Presence and Publishing
- Studio X
- Commerce Net

Figure 4.1: Gary Welz's home page (Continued)

- Internet Shopping Network
- Ogilvy and Mather
- Net Market Company
- Downtown Anywhere

Just Cool Sites:

- WebWorld
- Cybersight
- Science Television

Gary Welz, gary@setn.org

Figure 4.1: Gary Welz's home page (Continued)

EXAMPLE 2—A VIEWER INTEREST SURVEY

One of Gary Welz's projects is the Science and Engineering Television Network (SETN). He's created the viewer interest survey used for this example. It can be found at http://www.service.com/stv/survey.html. You can get there from his home page by first linking to SETN's home page at http://www.service.com/-stv/setncall.html. This is a good example of a form. It begins with an introduction describing the purpose of the form and what will be done with the input information. Then the form itself is divided into two parts by horizontal rules. Radio buttons and checkboxes are used almost exclusively for the readers' input.

The HTML code begins with a head containing the title of the page and a base tag to resolve relative addresses, such as the URL /cgi-bin/survey.pl, which is specified as the value of the ACTION attribute in the initial FORM tag. This allows the form to be copied to different servers while ensuring that the input will be processed by the original server script, http://www.service.com/stv/cgi-bin/survey.pl.

The <FORM></FORM> tags appear immediately inside of the <BODY></BODY> tags. Actually, the starting FORM tag could have been placed later in the file, just as long as it appeared before any input objects. The ACTION and METHOD attributes specify that the reader's input should be posted to a script, survey.pl, in the cgi-bin directory.

```
<HEAD>
<TITLE>Science and Engineering Television Network Survey</TITLE>
<BASE HREF="http://www.service.com/stv/survey.html">
</HEAD>

<BODY>
<FORM ACTION="/cgi-bin/survey.pl" METHOD=POST>
```

EXAMPLE 2—A VIEWER INTEREST SURVEY **65**

```
<H2>Science and Engineering Television Network</H2>
<H1>Viewing Interest Survey</H1>

(Note -- the purpose of this survey is to assess the level of interest in a
proposed video service; your response will not be used as or be considered a
commitment to purchase any equipment or services described in this survey.)
<P>
The Science and Engineering Television Network, Inc.  (SETN), a non-profit
consortium of scientific and engineering societies is planning to launch a regular
international video service of 2 - 4 hours per week beginning early in 1995.  This
service would be delivered to viewers at home or office locations in North America
via a direct broadcast satellite service.  Viewers in other regions will also be
offered the service via satellite if interest is sufficient.
<P>
Proposed programming will consist of:
<UL>
<LI>News capsules and announcements with leading science journalists
<LI>Presentations of current research developments
<LI>Live discussions/interviews -- focusing on authors in "hot" research areas
<LI>New techniques, equipment, hardware, software for laboratories
<LI>Where research grants are and how to get them
<LI>Computer applications in specific disciplines
<LI>Timely features -- pending legislation, newmakers, industry reports
<LI>Events at the NSF, Institute of Medicine and National Academies of Science and
Engineering
<LI>Reports from Government Labs about their current activities
<LI>Television analogs of print publications, e.g. Communications of the ACM,
Physics Today
</UL>
<P>
SETN will create supplements to programming that will be made available on the
Internet and regularly solicit the opinions and suggestions of viewers via the
Internet.
<P>
Click here if you would like more <A HREF=http://www.service.com/stv/setncall.html>
information about SETN</A>, its participating organizations and its proposed
programming.  We also invite other organizations to provide SETN programming,
assist in distribution and sponsor programs.
<PRE>

</PRE>
<BR>
```

The section of HTML code above ends with preformatting tags <PRE></PRE>,
containing a couple of extra carriage returns to add some space after the introduc-
tory text and before the form proper. This is the correct way to add white space.
Using multiple <P> tags will not work with most browsers; the extra <P> tags are

ignored. At the very end of the section is a line break tag, <BR>. My guess is that this is a mistake—Gary probably wanted to use a horizontal rule here.

The 14 questions of the survey form are formatted using a definition list; each question is formatted with a definition term tag, <DT>. Since there are no matching definition description (<DD>) tags, this is not strictly good HTML. It's a common fudge and has the useful effect of indenting and separating multiple sets of paragraphs. Other list structures such as OL, UL, and MENU can be used to indent a set of paragraphs; however, these structures are not meant to handle multiple paragraphs per list item and have the undesirable effect of decorating your text with numbers or bullets. <BLOCKQUOTE></BLOCKQUOTE> will also indent sets of paragraphs, but will also put the text into italics with some browsers. Likewise, <PRE></PRE> will render the text with a typewriter font. There are several proposals for additional HTML tags such as <INDENT> </INDENT> and <CENTER></CENTER> to control the relative positioning of paragraphs and other structures on a page. Until such tags are adopted, fudges like this use of definition tags will continue to be used.

None of the radio buttons or checkboxes has a default value specified. Each set of radio buttons on this form has the number of its associated question specified as the value of the NAME attribute defining the button set, and the label of each radio button is used for the VALUE attribute. For example, if in question 1A you selected the button labeled *Not at all* and in question 1B selected *Somewhat*, then the script would see 1A=notatall&1B=somewhat&… in the input stream. This is an easy way to keep track of which answers go with which questions.

The checkboxes in question 9 have names that are abbreviations of their legends. The matching VALUE attributes have the same values if checked. If, for example, you checked *American Chemical Society* and *American Physical Society* and left all the other checkboxes blank, then the script for the checkbox section would have

```
aaas=&acs=acs&ams=&aps=aps&asm=&acn=&ieee=&9=&other9="
```

in its input for that portion of the form.

```
If your WWW browser does not allow you to fill out this questionnaire, we urge you
to send your answers via email to: gary@setn.org.  You may also print out the
survey and mail your response to the address given on the SETN info pages.
<P>
<DL>
<DT>1A) For residents of North America:  SETN will be available in North America
via direct broadcast satellite on a subscription basis.  Would you be interested
in viewing this service if it were available.
<BR>
<INPUT TYPE="radio" NAME="1A" VALUE="notatall">Not at all
```

EXAMPLE 2—A VIEWER INTEREST SURVEY   **67**

```
<INPUT TYPE="radio" NAME="1A" VALUE="somewhat">Somewhat
<INPUT TYPE="radio" NAME="1A" VALUE="very">Very
<P>
<DT>1B) For residents of regions other than North America:  SETN may soon be made
available via satellite and other means to scientists and engineers in other
regions.  Would you be interested in viewing this service if it were available.
<BR>
<INPUT TYPE="radio" NAME="1B" VALUE="notatall">Not at all
<INPUT TYPE="radio" NAME="1B" VALUE="somewhat">Somewhat
<INPUT TYPE="radio" NAME="1B" VALUE="very">Very
<P>
<DT>2)If you were a subscriber, would you prefer to view this service at your:
<BR>
<INPUT TYPE="radio" NAME="2" VALUE="home">Home
<INPUT TYPE="radio" NAME="2" VALUE="office">Office
<INPUT TYPE="radio" NAME="2" VALUE="lab">Lab
<INPUT TYPE="radio" NAME="2" VALUE="campus">Campus
<P>
<DT>3) What time of day would you prefer to watch?
<BR>
<INPUT TYPE="radio" NAME="3" VALUE="morning">Morning
<INPUT TYPE="radio" NAME="3" VALUE="afternoon">Afternoon
<INPUT TYPE="radio" NAME="3" VALUE="evening">Evening
<P>
<DT>4) What general area of programming would you be most interested in viewing
<BR>
<INPUT TYPE="radio" NAME="4" VALUE="biology" >Biology/Biochemistry
<INPUT TYPE="radio" NAME="4" VALUE="chemistry" >Chemistry
<INPUT TYPE="radio" NAME="4" VALUE="physics" >Physics
<INPUT TYPE="radio" NAME="4" VALUE="mathematics" >Mathematics
<BR>
<INPUT TYPE="radio" NAME="4" VALUE="computer science" >Computer science
<INPUT TYPE="radio" NAME="4" VALUE="elec engineering" >
Electrical Engineering/Electronic Engineering
<BR>
<INPUT TYPE="radio" NAME="4" VALUE="earth and atmospheric sciences">
Earth and Atmospheric Sciences
<INPUT TYPE="radio" NAME="4" VALUE="astronomy and astrophysics">
Astronomy and Astrophysics
<BR>
<INPUT TYPE="radio" NAME="4" VALUE="other engineering" >
Other Engineering
<INPUT TYPE="radio" NAME="4" VALUE="science policy" >
Science Policy
<P>
<HR>
In order to obtain SETN in North America, you or your employer must obtain direct
```

broadcast satellite receive equipment, which consists of an 18" antenna and
converter. This equipment, which can be self-installed, will cost approximately
$700; it can be obtained on a lease basis for approximately $25 per month.
<P>
(Other programming will be available on an optional - not required - basis; this
programming includes virtually all current cable TV channel, including such
business and information channels as CNN and CNBC.)
<P>
<DT>5) Would you consider obtaining the direct broadcast satellite equipment or
requesting that your employer do so for your office, lab or department?

<INPUT TYPE="radio" NAME="5" VALUE="yes">Yes
<INPUT TYPE="radio" NAME="5" VALUE="no">No
<P>
<DT>6) What do you think would be a reasonable monthly subscription price for you
or your employer to pay for SETN?

<INPUT TYPE="radio" NAME="6" VALUE="under5">Under $5 per month
<INPUT TYPE="radio" NAME="6" VALUE="5_10">$5 - $10 per month

<INPUT TYPE="radio" NAME="6" VALUE="11_15">$11 - $15 per month
<INPUT TYPE="radio" NAME="6" VALUE="16_20">$16 - $20 per month
<P>
<DT>7) What would be your reaction if 5 -10 minutes of commercial advertising for
scientific instruments, computer hardware/software, scientific publications,
events, et. al. were shown every hour?

<INPUT TYPE="radio" NAME="7" VALUE="interested">I would be interested if they were
relevant (appropriate for this audience)

<INPUT TYPE="radio" NAME="7" VALUE="neutral">They wouldn't bother me, but I
probably wouldn't watch them

<INPUT TYPE="radio" NAME="7" VALUE="object">I would object to their presence.
<P>
<DT>8) I am currently a

<INPUT TYPE="radio" NAME="8" VALUE="graduate">
Graduate/undergraduate student
<INPUT TYPE="radio" NAME="8" VALUE="phd" >
Ph.D. scientist or engineer

<INPUT TYPE="radio" NAME="8" VALUE="nonphd">
Non-Ph.D. scientist or engineer
<INPUT TYPE="radio" NAME="8" VALUE="other">
Other <INPUT NAME="other8" SIZE=20>
<P>

Example 2—A viewer interest survey **69**

```
<DT>9) I belong to the:
<BR>
<INPUT TYPE="checkbox" NAME="aaas" VALUE="aaas" >
American Association for the Advancement of Science
<BR>
<INPUT TYPE="checkbox" NAME="acs" VALUE="acs" >
American Chemical Society
<BR>
<INPUT TYPE="checkbox" NAME="ams" VALUE="ams">
American Mathematical Society
<BR>
<INPUT TYPE="checkbox" NAME="aps" VALUE="aps">
American Physical Society
<BR>
<INPUT TYPE="checkbox" NAME="asm" VALUE="asm">
American Society of Microbiology
<BR>
<INPUT TYPE="checkbox" NAME="acm" VALUE="acm">
Association for Computing Machinery
<BR>
<INPUT TYPE="checkbox" NAME="ieee" VALUE="ieee">
IEEE or another engineering society
<BR>
<INPUT TYPE="checkbox"  NAME="9" VALUE="other">
Some other Professional Society <INPUT NAME="other9" SIZE=20>
<P>
<DT>10) I live on what continent
<BR>
<INPUT TYPE="radio" NAME="10" VALUE="na">North America
<INPUT TYPE="radio" NAME="10" VALUE="sa">South America
<INPUT TYPE="radio" NAME="10" VALUE="europe">Europe
<INPUT TYPE="radio" NAME="10" VALUE="asia">Asia or Australia
<BR>
<INPUT TYPE="radio" NAME="10" VALUE="africa">Africa
<INPUT TYPE="radio" NAME="10" VALUE="other">Other
<INPUT TYPE="text" NAME="other10" SIZE=20>
<P>
<DT>11) My current annual income category is:
<BR>
<INPUT TYPE="radio" NAME="11" VALUE="20k">
Less than $20,000
<INPUT TYPE="radio" NAME="11" VALUE="20k_50k">
Between $20,000 and $50,000
<BR>
<INPUT TYPE="radio" NAME="11" VALUE="50k_80K">
Between $50,000 and $80,000
<INPUT TYPE="radio" NAME="11" VALUE="80k">
```

```
More than $80,000
<BR>
<INPUT TYPE="radio" NAME="11" VALUE="none">
Prefer not to answer
<P>
<DT>12) Comments, programming ideas, suggestions, questions about SETN:
<BR>
<INPUT NAME="comments" SIZE=60>
<P>
<DT>13) Respondent Information
<BR>
<INPUT NAME="name" SIZE=40> Name
<BR>
<INPUT NAME="street" SIZE=40> Street
<BR>
<INPUT NAME="city" SIZE=40> City, State, Zip
<BR>
<INPUT NAME="email" SIZE=40> Email addresss
<BR>
<INPUT NAME="phone" SIZE=40> Phone
<BR>
<INPUT NAME="fax" SIZE=40> Fax
<P>
<DT>14) Please send me more information about direct broadcast television services
(North America only) and  the SETN service.
<BR>
<INPUT TYPE="radio" NAME="14" VALUE="yes">Yes
<INPUT TYPE="radio" NAME="14" VALUE="no">No
</DL>
<P>
<HR>
<INPUT TYPE="submit" VALUE="Submit Survey">
<INPUT TYPE="reset" VALUE="Clear Information">
<P>
<HR>
If you have questions, please send e-mail to: gary@setn.org
</FORM>
</BODY>
```

Question 13 above asks for respondent information with a set of six input fields each 40 characters in size. Line breaks, <BR>, are used to separate the input lines. Instead of placing labels on the left of each field, which is usual for other applications that can present forms, Gary has placed the labels on the right. This technique aligns the input fields in a block without the bother of using preformated style tags. At the end of the form are the submit and reset buttons that should be part of every form. Here, the VALUE attribute is used to give the buttons names different than the default names of *Submit* and *Reset*.

EXAMPLE 2—A VIEWER INTEREST SURVEY **71**

Figure 4.2 shows how the Viewing Interest Survey Web page generated by this HTML code will look when displayed and printed using NCSA Mosaic. This page was created by Gary Welz.

Science and Engineering Television Network

Viewing Interest Survey

(Note -- the purpose of this survey is to assess the level of interest in a proposed video service; your response will not be used as or be considered a commitment to purchase any equipment or services described in this survey.)

The Science and Engineering Television Network, Inc. (SETN), a non-profit consortium of scientific and engineering societies is planning to launch a regular international video service of 2 - 4 hours per week beginning early in 1995. This service would be delivered to viewers at home or office locations in North America via a direct broadcast satellite service. Viewers in other regions will also be offered the service via satellite if interest is sufficient.

Proposed programming will consist of:
- News capsules and announcements with leading science journalists
- Presentations of current research developments
- Live discussions/interviews -- focusing on authors in "hot" research areas
- New techniques, equipment, hardware, software for laboratories
- Where research grants are and how to get them
- Computer applications in specific disciplines
- Timely features -- pending legislation, newmakers, industry reports
- Events at the NSF, Institute of Medicine and National Academies of Science and Engineering
- Reports from Government Labs about their current activities
- Television analogs of print publications, e.g. Communications of the ACM, Physics Today

SETN will create supplements to programming that will be made available on the Internet and regularly solicit the opinions and suggestions of viewers via the Internet.

Click here if you would like more information about SETN, its participating organizations and its proposed programming. We also invite other organizations to provide SETN programming, assist in distribution and sponsor programs.

If your WWW browser does not allow you to fill out this questionnaire, we urge you to send your answers via email to: gary@setn.org. You may also print out the survey and mail your response to the address given on the SETN info pages.

1A) For residents of North America: SETN will be available in North America via direct broadcast satellite on a subscription basis. Would you be interested in viewing this service if it were available.

O Not at all O Somewhat O Very

1B) For residents of regions other than North America: SETN may soon be made available via satellite and other means to scientists and engineers in other regions. Would you be interested in viewing this service if it were available.

O Not at all O Somewhat O Very

Figure 4.2: The Viewing Interest Survey

2)If you were a subscriber, would you prefer to view this service at your:
○ Home ○ Office ○ Lab ○ Campus

3) What time of day would you prefer to watch?
○ Morning ○ Afternoon ○ Evening

4) What general area of programming would you be most interested in viewing
○ Biology/Biochemistry ○ Chemistry ○ Physics ○ Mathematics
○ Computer science ○ Electrical Engineering/Electronic Engineering
○ Earth and Atmospheric Sciences ⦿ Astronomy and Astrophysics
○ Other Engineering ○ Science Policy

In order to obtain SETN in North America, you or your employer must obtain direct broadcast satellite receive equipment, which consists of an 18" antenna and converter. This equipment, which can be self-installed, will cost approximately $700; it can be obtained on a lease basis for approximately $25 per month.

(Other programming will be available on an optional - not required - basis; this programming includes virtually all current cable TV channel, including such business and information channels as CNN and CNBC.)

5) Would you consider obtaining the direct broadcast satellite equipment or requesting that your employer do so for your office, lab or department?
○ Yes ○ No

6) What do you think would be a reasonable monthly subscription price for you or your employer to pay for SETN?
○ Under $5 per month ○ $5 - $10 per month
○ $11 - $15 per month ○ $16 - $20 per month

7) What would be your reaction if 5 -10 minutes of commercial advertising for scientific instruments, computer hardware/software, scientific publications, events, et. al. were shown every hour?
○ I would be interested if they were relevant (appropriate for this audience)

○ They wouldn't bother me, but I probably wouldn't watch them

○ I would object to their presence.

8) I am currently a
○ Graduate/undergraduate student ○ Ph.D. scientist or engineer
○ Non-Ph.D. scientist or engineer ○ Other [_____]

9) I belong to the:

Figure 4.2: The Viewing Interest Survey (Continued)

Example 2—A viewer interest survey **73**

☐ American Association for the Advancement of Science

☐ American Chemical Society

☐ American Mathematical Society

☐ American Physical Society

☐ American Society of Microbiology

☐ Association for Computing Machinery

☐ IEEE or another engineering society

☐ Some other Professional Society [_____]

10) I live on what continent

○ North America ○ South America ○ Europe ○ Asia or Australia

○ Africa ○ Other [_____]

11) My current annual income category is:

○ Less than $20,000 ○ Between $20,000 and $50,000

○ Between $50,000 and $80,000 ○ More than $80,000

○ Prefer not to answer

12) Comments, programming ideas, suggestions, questions about SETN:

[_____]

13) Respondent Information

[_____] Name

[_____] Street

[_____] City, State, Zip

[_____] Email addresss

[_____] Phone

[_____] Fax

14) Please send me more information about direct broadcast television services (North America only) and the SETN service.

○ Yes ○ No

(Submit Survey) (Clear Information)

If you have questions, please send e-mail to: gary@setn.org

Figure 4.2: The Viewing Interest Survey (Continued)

EXAMPLE 3—A SMALL ORGANIZATION'S HOME PAGE

The New Jersey Macintosh User's Group (NJMUG) provides this World Wide Web site as a service to its members and the Macintosh user community at large. Most of the page is a collection of links to resources of interest to Macintosh users. The links are organized into sections separated by horizontal rules. Each section consists of strongly emphasized text followed by an unordered list. I don't know if it was intentional, but there's not a single heading tag used in the entire document; nevertheless, I feel this is a very nice organization of information and references. The NJMUG home page was developed by Steven Hatch, Creative Director of The Turnaround Team, Inc. The URL of the page is http://www.intac.com/njmug/njmug.html.

Steven's HTML code starts with a head section containing the page's title and an authorship link as well as some comments to identify the HTML file should it be viewed out of context. The top of the page begins with an image, njmug_logo.gif, from a subdirectory called *images*. The image itself is an anchor for a link to a sound file with the URL http://www.intac.com/njmug/-files/njmug.au. Clicking on the image will download the sound file and launch a helper application to play it. It is a recording of someone reading the welcome message. Following the first horizontal rule is an "under construction" disclaimer rendered with citation tags, <CITE></CITE>, containing an anchor on the word *note* with a mailto URL.

Some nonstandard attributes are specified in the <IMG> tag that points to the NJMUG logo. The HEIGHT and WIDTH attributes act to reserve space for the image in order to speed up page formatting. The ALIGN attribute with the value *left* instructs the browser to align the image to the left of the paragraph containing it. These attributes are currently recognized only by Netscape Communications's browser, Netscape, and are ignored by all others that I know of.

The page also uses font tags, <FONT></FONT>, to specify a type size slightly larger than the default size. This is also a Netscape–only feature. If you have this browser, you might want to compare its display of these nonstandard elements to that of NCSA's Mosaic.

```
<HTML>
<HEAD>
<TITLE>NJ Macintosh Users Group Web</TITLE>
<!-- OWNER_NAME="Steven Hatch" -->
<LINK rev=made HREF="mailto:hatch@turnaround.com">
```

EXAMPLE 3—A SMALL ORGANIZATION'S HOME PAGE **75**

```
<!-- OWNER_INFO="The Turnaround Team, Inc., Westfield, NJ, 07090" -->
</HEAD>

<BODY>
<A HREF="http://www.intac.com/njmug/files/njmug.au">
<IMG SRC="images/njmug_logo.gif" ALIGN=left HSPACE=6 WIDTH=250 HEIGHT=100
ALT="NJMUG "></A>
<STRONG><FONT size=+1>Welcome to the NJMUG Web</FONT></STRONG><Br>
This site is a service of the New Jersey Macintosh Users Group.
<HR>
<CITE>
This site will always be under construction. If you have any comments, suggestions
or additions to this site, please drop me a
<A HREF="mailto:hatch@turnaround.com">note.</A>
</CITE><Br>
<HR>
<A HREF= "whats-new.html">
<IMG ALIGN=MIDDLE SRC="images/at-icon.gif" HSPACE=6 WIDTH=32 HEIGHT=32 ALT="@ Icon
"> <STRONG>What's NEW at the NJMUG WWW?</STRONG></A>


<HR>
<STRONG>NJMUG Info:</STRONG>
<UL>
<LI> <A HREF= "njmug-info.html">About NJMUG and Membership Info</A>
<LI> <A HREF= "njmug_bbs.html">NJMUG's BBS</A>
<LI> <B><A HREF= "njmug-bbs-news.html">NJMUG's BBS News Flash</A></b> (NEW)
<LI> <A HREF= "meeting_info.html">
Find out about the upcoming NJMUG meeting.</A>
</UL>
<HR>
<STRONG>Macintosh Internet sites:</STRONG>
<UL>
<LI> <A HREF= "http://www.apple.com/">Apple Computer WWW Server</A>
<LI> <A HREF= "http://www.info.apple.com/">
Apple Support and Information Web Site</A>
<LI> <A HREF= "http://power.globalnews.com/">
PowerPC News Electronic Magazine</A>
<LI> <A HREF= "http://web.nexor.co.uk/mac-archive/mac-archive.html">Macintosh
Archive--a great way to search for files</A>
<LI> <A HREF= "http://hyperarchive.lcs.mit.edu/HyperArchive.html">
HyperArchive--the best way to browse info-mac</A>
<LI> <A HREF= "http://ici.proper.com/1/mac">Macintosh Index</A>
</UL>
<HR>
<STRONG>Apple's Official FTP Sites:</STRONG>
```

```
<UL>
<LI> <A HREF= "ftp://ftp.apple.com/dts/mac/">Developer Technical Support</A>
<LI> <A HREF= "ftp://atg.apple.com/">Apple's Technology Group</A>
<LI> <A HREF= "ftp://ftp.austin.apple.com/">Apple Austin Texas</A>
<LI> <A HREF= "ftp://abs.apple.com/abs/">Apple's Business Systems</A>
<LI> <A HREF= "ftp://seeding.apple.com/">Apple Seeding</A>
<LI> <A HREF= "ftp://gaea.kgs.ukans.edu/applescript/">
AppleScript Developer Utilities</A>
<LI> <A HREF= "files/mac-ftp-sites-388.html">
Macintosh FTP Sites List</A>
</UL>
<HR>
<STRONG>Macintosh Internet Information and Configurations:</STRONG>
<UL>
<LI> <A HREF= "files/MACSLIP.TXT">
<B>MacSLIP Frequently Asked Questions</b></A> (NEW)
<LI> <A HREF= "files/INTAC.script">
MacSLIP Connection Script</A> for
<A HREF= "http://www.intac.com/">INTAC</A>
<LI> <A HREF= "internet_install.html">
InterSLIP Installer Application</A> for
<A HREF= "http://www.intac.com/">INTAC</A>
<LI> <A HREF= "files/INTAC-Gateway-Script">InterSLIP Gateway Script</A> for <A
HREF= "http://www.intac.com/">INTAC</A>
<LI> <A HREF= "files/scr-interslip-dial-script">
InterSLIP Dial Script</A> for
<A HREF= "http://www.intac.com/">INTAC</A>
<LI> <A HREF= "http://www.intac.com/~jvafai/macppp_tcp.html">
MacTCP & MacPPP Configuration</A> for
<A HREF= "http://www.intac.com/">INTAC</A>--<I>by Jonathan Vafai</I></A>
<LI> <A HREF= "http://www.iia.org/~walld/TIA_Config.html">
The Internet Adaptor Configuration (TIA)</A>
for IIA--<I>by Dennis Wall</I>
<LI> <A HREF= "file:/ftp.tidbits.com/pub/tidbits/dominating-mactcp-
draft.etx">Dominating MacTCP</A>--<I>by Adam Engst</I>
<LI> <A HREF= "http://rever.nmsu.edu/~elharo/faq/faqs.html">
Macintosh Frequently Asked Questions</A>--<I>by Elliotte Harold</I>
</UL>
<HR>
<STRONG>Macintosh Internet Software:</STRONG>
<UL>
<LI> <A HREF= "ftp://ftp.qualcomm.com/quest/mac/eudora/">
Eudora Mail Application</A>
<LI> <A HREF= "ftp://ftp.intac.com/pub/mac/mactcp/news/">
Usenet News Readers</A>
```

EXAMPLE 3—A SMALL ORGANIZATION'S HOME PAGE **77**

```
<LI> <A HREF= "ftp://ftp.intac.com/pub/mac/mactcp/gopher/">
Gopher Clients</A>
<LI> <A HREF= "ftp://ftp.intac.com/pub/mac/mactcp/ftp/">
FTP & Archie Clients</A>
<LI> <A HREF= "ftp://ftp.intac.com/pub/mac/mactcp/web/">
WWW Clients (Mosaic & MacWeb)</A>
<LI> <A HREF= "ftp://ftp.intac.com/pub/mac/mactcp/misc/">WAIS Client</A>
<LI> <A HREF= "ftp://ftp.intac.com/pub/mac/mactcp/telnet/">
Telnet Application</A>
<LI> <A HREF= "ftp://ftp.intac.com/pub/mac/mactcp/drivers/">
PPP & SLIP Drivers</A>
</UL>
<HR>
<STRONG>Macintosh USENET Newsgroups:</STRONG>
<UL>
<LI> <A HREF="news:comp.sys.mac.advocacy">comp.sys.mac.advocacy</A>
<LI> <A HREF="news:comp.sys.mac.announce">comp.sys.mac.announce</A>
<LI> <A HREF="news:comp.sys.mac.apps">comp.sys.mac.apps</A>
<LI> <A HREF="news:comp.sys.mac.comm">comp.sys.mac.comm</A>
<LI> <A HREF="news:comp.sys.mac.digest">comp.sys.mac.digest</A>
<LI> <A HREF="news:comp.sys.mac.games">comp.sys.mac.games</A>
<LI> <A HREF="news:comp.sys.mac.graphics">comp.sys.mac.graphics</A>
<LI> <A HREF="news:comp.sys.mac.hardware">comp.sys.mac.hardware</A>
<LI> <A HREF="news:comp.sys.mac.misc">comp.sys.mac.misc</A>
<LI> <A HREF="news:comp.sys.mac.portables">comp.sys.mac.portables</A>
<LI> <A HREF="news:comp.sys.mac.programmer">comp.sys.mac.programmer</A>
<LI> <A HREF="news:comp.sys.mac.scitech">comp.sys.mac.scitech</A>
<LI> <A HREF="news:comp.sys.mac.system">comp.sys.mac.system</A>
<LI> <A HREF="news:comp.sys.mac.wanted">comp.sys.mac.wanted</A>
</UL>
<HR>
<ADDRESS>
Last updated by <A HREF= "http://www.intac.com/turnaround/hatch.html">
Steven Hatch</A> (hatch@turnaround.com) on OCT-31-94
</ADDRESS>
</BODY>
</HTML>
```

Figure 4.3 shows how the Web page generated by this HTML code will look when displayed and printed using NCSA Mosaic.

**Welcome to the NJMUG Web**
This site is a service of the New Jersey Macintosh Users Group.

This site will always be under construction. If you have any comments, suggestions or additions to this site, please drop me a note.

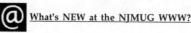 **What's NEW at the NJMUG WWW?**

NJMUG Info:
- About NJMUG and Membership Info
- NJMUG's BBS
- **NJMUG's BBS News Flash** (NEW)
- Find out about the upcoming NJMUG meeting.

Macintosh Internet sites:
- Apple Computer WWW Server
- Apple Support and Information Web Site
- PowerPC News Electronic Magazine
- Macintosh Archive--a great way to search for files
- HyperArchive--the best way to browse info-mac
- Macintosh Index

Apple's Official FTP Sites:
- Developer Technical Support
- Apple's Technology Group
- Apple Austin Texas
- Apple's Business Systems
- Apple Seeding
- AppleScript Developer Utilities
- Macintosh FTP Sites List

Macintosh Internet Information and Configurations:
- **MacSLIP Frequently Asked Questions** (NEW)
- MacSLIP Connection Script for INTAC

New Jersey Macintosh Users Group Web Pages <http://www.intac.com/njmug/> ©1994 Steven Hatch.

Figure 4.3: NJMUG home page

EXAMPLE 4—A BROCHURE **79**

- InterSLIP Installer Application for INTAC
- InterSLIP Gateway Script for INTAC
- InterSLIP Dial Script for INTAC
- MacTCP & MacPPP Configuration for INTAC--*by Jonathan Vafai*

The Internet Adaptor Configuration (TIA) for IIA--*by Dennis Wall* Dominating MacTCP--*by Adam Engst* Macintosh Frequently Asked Questions--*by Elliotte Harold*

Macintosh Internet Software:
- Eudora Mail Application
- Usenet News Readers
- Gopher Clients
- FTP & Archie Clients
- WWW Clients (Mosaic & MacWeb)
- WAIS Client
- Telnet Application
- PPP & SLIP Drivers

Macintosh USENET Newsgroups:
- comp.sys.mac.advocacy
- comp.sys.mac.announce
- comp.sys.mac.apps
- comp.sys.mac.comm
- comp.sys.mac.digest
- comp.sys.mac.games
- comp.sys.mac.graphics
- comp.sys.mac.hardware
- comp.sys.mac.misc
- comp.sys.mac.portables
- comp.sys.mac.programmer
- comp.sys.mac.scitech
- comp.sys.mac.system
- comp.sys.mac.wanted

Last updated by Steven Hatch (hatch@turnaround.com) on OCT-31-94

Figure 4.3: NJMUG home page (Continued)

EXAMPLE 4—A BROCHURE

This is another example of Steven Hatch's work, a brochure describing the communication services offered by his company, the Turnaround Team. This page is at the URL http://www.intac.com/turnaround/Communications.html. It displays a good mixture of techniques—an icon-based menu section, text paragraphs and list structures. There are a few mistakes in the HTML that generates this page; nevertheless, it's a good-looking Web page with well-organized content.

The body of the page begins with the logo of the Turnaround Team followed by a repeat of the page title, *Communication Services,* set with strong emphasis using the tags <STRONG></STRONG>. This text is also enclosed in font tags, <FONT></FONT> with the SIZE attribute specifying that the text should be rendered in a font two sizes larger than the default size. The font tags, as you can see from the generated page, are not recognized by NCSA Mosaic.

After the first horizontal rule is an icon-based menu with seven choices. Each choice is represented by an icon image and a label describing the choice, both of which are enclosed in anchor tags containing the link information. The image tags for the icons specify HEIGHT and WIDTH attributes. These are recognized by some browsers and can make in-line image loading much faster. The entire menu section is enclosed in two sets of style tags. The innermost set specifies the preformatted style with the <PRE></PRE> tags to position the choices into two columns. The text for the first, third, and fifth icon labels have extra spaces appended to them, which the preformatting style preserves. The outer style tags specify that strong emphasis should be applied to all of the labels. When rendered in NCSA Mosaic, however, the preformatted style overrides the strong style and the labels appear in a plain-text typewriter-style font with no emphasis applied. I think a better way to construct this section would be to keep the <STRONG></STRONG> tags where they are and use the <PRE></PRE> tags only for the additional spaces needed to align the icons, as in this variation of Stephen's HTML code:

```
<A HREF= "Interactive.html">
<IMG ALIGN=top SRC="images/interactive-icon.gif" ALT="Interactive Icon">
Interactive Brochures</A>
<PRE>           </PRE><A HREF= "Ultimate_Secret.HTML">
<IMG ALIGN=top SRC="images/sales-icon.gif" ALT="Sales Game Icon">
Sales Games</A>
```

This way, in all browsers, the labels would appear in the default paragraph text style with strong emphasis. The page below begins with a starting <HTML> tag.

```
<HTML>
<HEAD>
<TITLE>Communication Services</TITLE>
</HEAD>

<BODY>
<IMG SRC="images/TTT_logo.gif" ALIGN=left HSPACE=3 WIDTH=185 HEIGHT=60 ALT="The
Turnaround Team, Inc.">
<STRONG>
<FONT SIZE=+2>  Communication Services</FONT>
</STRONG><BR>
In the past few years, The Turnaround Team has been on the cutting-edge of
computer-based, interactive multimedia and online communications.
```

Example 4—A brochure   **81**

```
<BR>

<HR>
<STRONG>
<PRE>
<A HREF= "Interactive.html">
<IMG ALIGN=top SRC="images/interactive-icon.gif" WIDTH=99 HEIGHT=65
ALT="Interactive Icon"> Interactive Brochures</A>
<A HREF= "Ultimate_Secret.HTML">
<IMG ALIGN=top SRC="images/sales-icon.gif" WIDTH=99 HEIGHT=65 ALT="Sales Game
Icon"> Sales Games</A>
<A HREF= "Postal_Modern_Art.html">
<IMG ALIGN=top SRC="images/training-icon.gif" WIDTH=99 HEIGHT=65 ALT="Training
Icon"> Interactive Training</A>
<A HREF= "http://www.intac.com/turnaround/OWL/">
<IMG ALIGN=top SRC="images/online-icon.gif" WIDTH=99 HEIGHT=65 ALT="Online Icon">
Online Services</A>
<A HREF= "CustomNet/CustomNet.html">
<IMG ALIGN=top SRC="images/presentations-icon.gif" WIDTH=99 HEIGHT=65
ALT="Presentations Icon"> Presentations</A>
<A HREF= "boc-semicon.html">
<IMG ALIGN=top SRC="images/kiosks-icon.gif" WIDTH=99 HEIGHT=65 ALT="Online Icon">
Kiosks</A>
<A HREF= "isp-cdf.html">
<IMG ALIGN=top SRC="images/simulations-icon.gif" WIDTH=99 HEIGHT=65
ALT="Simulations Icon"> Simulations</A>
</PRE>
</STRONG>
```

The remaining sections of the page are fairly straightforward HTML code with headings, paragraphs, and lists. Explicit style tags—<B> for bold and <I> for italics—are used in the section with the heading *A Proven Methodology.* These style choices were probably made to duplicate the exact look of a preexisting printed version of the brochure. This approach can be a losing strategy, as one can only duplicate the look with one's own browser, without any guarantees about what the page will look like with anyone else's. Headings would have done just as well to convey the relationships of the items. Note the two paragraph marks after the second paragraph of text and just before the horizontal rule. These extra paragraph marks will be ignored by most browsers. Note also that the corporate name *AT&T* must be specified as *AT&T* with a character entity for the ampersand.

```
<HR>
<H2>Multimedia Presentations</H2>
In the past few years, The Turnaround Team has been on the cutting-edge of
```

computer-based, interactive multimedia communication. The Team is a certified
developer for Apple Computer as well as Macromedia, the world's leading developer
of multimedia software programs.
```
<P>
```
The Team's computer skills, combined with its approach to solving marketing
problems, have resulted in a number of extraordinary presentations --
extraordinary in their impact and in their effectiveness.
```
<P><P>
<HR>
<H2>Examples of Interactive Multimedia</H2>
<H3>Interactive Brochures</H3>
<UL>
<LI> <A HREF= "Interactive.html">Turnaround Interactive</A><BR>
```
Check out The Turnaround Team's Interactive Brochure.
```
<LI> <A HREF= "Ultimate_Secret.HTML">
```
Ultimate_Secret--Turnaround's promo game!</A>
This is The Turnaround Team's interactive promo adventure game.
```
<LI> <A HREF= "Postal_Modern_Art.html">
```
USPS Postal Modern Art--A Quick Study in Postal Modern Art</A>
The US Postal Services' Postal Modern Art interactive training disk.
```
<LI> <A HREF= "CustomNet/CustomNet.html">AT&amp;T CustomNet GOLD</A><BR>
```
This is an example of an interactive brochure created for AT&T.
```
</UL>
<HR>
<H2>
```
A Proven Methodology</H2>
Whether involved in a major turnaround effort or in the creation of a single
multimedia communication, The Turnaround Team applies the methodology Steve Most
has developed and refined over the past 25 years.
```
<B><I>
<P>
```
The three hallmarks of The Turnaround Team's methodology are:
```
</I>
<P>
```
1)   Thorough research, both inside and outside the company. </B>
```
<P>
```
All projects begin with a review of existing research, past communications, and
personal interviews. Depending on the project, formal quantitative and qualitative
methods may be recommended. Our goal is to uncover the key aspects of the buying
decision for the product or service.<B>
```
<P>
```
2)   A team approach. </B>
```
<P>
```
Our methodology brings every member of the team, including the client, onto the
project from the very beginning. This assures that the final communication will
always reflect the key aspects of the buying decision.<I></I><B>
```
<P>
```

EXAMPLE 4—A BROCHURE   **83**

```
3)    Managing a project through implementation. </B>
<P>
Unlike typical consultants, The Turnaround Team, through its creative department,
helps to fully implement the required communications, whether they are TV
commercials, magazine ads, direct-mail catalogs, or interactive multimedia
presentations.
```

The last part of the page is a set of statements organized by a menu list and introduced by text in bold italics. Following the menu is an anchor with an icon and label to take the reader back to Turnaround's home page. Following that is the page signature in <ADDRESS></ADDRESS> tags with a link to the author's personal home page.

```
<B><I>
<P>
The Team's methodology has been successful in a variety of business situations,
including:</I></B>
<MENU>
<LI>Businesses that are doing well, but nowhere near the potential that their
plans projected.
<LI>Ventures that lose their momentum after initial success, despite a seemingly
good business proposition.
<LI>Businesses that are underachieving management's expectations.
<LI>Brands that are failing in test market, though expectations were very high.
<LI>Businesses whose strengths are being threatened by new competition.
<LI>Acquisitions of well-known but poorly performing businesses that need a growth
strategy to attain the objectives of the new owners.
</MENU>

<HR>
<A HREF= "http://www.intac.com/turnaround/">
<IMG ALIGN=middle SRC="images/TTT-logo-icon.gif" WIDTH=100 HEIGHT=32
ALT="Turnaround Icon"> Back to the Turnaround Home Page.</a>
<HR>
<ADDRESS>
Last updated by <A HREF= "http://www.intac.com/turnaround/hatch.html">
Steven Hatch</A> (hatch@turnaround.com) on NOV-01-94
</ADDRESS>
</BODY>
</HTML>
```

Figure 4.4 shows how this brochure looks when displayed and printed using NCSA Mosaic.

 Communication Services

In the past few years, The Turnaround Team has been on the cutting-edge of computer-based, interactive multimedia and online communications.

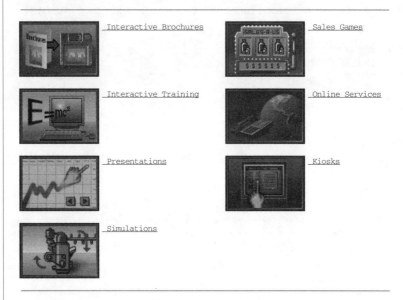

Multimedia Presentations

In the past few years, The Turnaround Team has been on the cutting-edge of computer-based, interactive multimedia communication. The Team is a certified developer for Apple Computer as well as Macromedia, the world's leading developer of multimedia software programs.

The Team's computer skills, combined with its approach to solving marketing problems, have resulted in a number of extraordinary presentations -- extraordinary in their impact and in their effectiveness.

Examples of Interactive Multimedia

Interactive Brochures

Figure 4.4: The Turnaround Team's brochure

EXAMPLE 4—A BROCHURE **85**

Turnaround Interactive

Check out The Turnaround Team's Interactive Brochure.

Ultimate Secret--Turnaround's promo game!

This is The Turnaround Team's interactive promo adventure game.

USPS Postal Modern Art--A Quick Study in Postal Modern Art

The US Postal Services' Postal Modern Art interactive training disk.

AT&T CustomNet GOLD

This is an example of an interactive brochure created for AT&T.

A Proven Methodology

Whether involved in a major turnaround effort or in the creation of a single multimedia communication, The Turnaround Team applies the methodology Steve Most has developed and refined over the past 25 years.

The three hallmarks of The Turnaround Team's methodology are:

1) Thorough research, both inside and outside the company.

All projects begin with a review of existing research, past communications, and personal interviews. Depending on the project, formal quantitative and qualitative methods may be recommended. Our goal is to uncover the key aspects of the buying decision for the product or service.

2) A team approach.

Our methodology brings every member of the team, including the client, onto the project from the very beginning. This assures that the final communication will always reflect the key aspects of the buying decision.

3) Managing a project through implementation.

Unlike typical consultants, The Turnaround Team, through its creative department, helps to fully implement the required communications, whether they are TV commercials, magazine ads, direct-mail catalogs, or interactive multimedia presentations.

The Team's methodology has been successful in a variety of business situations, including:

Businesses that are doing well, but nowhere near the potential that their plans projected.

Figure 4.4: The Turnaround Team's brochure (Continued)

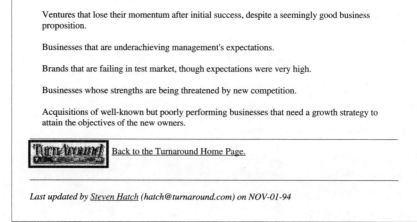

Ventures that lose their momentum after initial success, despite a seemingly good business proposition.

Businesses that are underachieving management's expectations.

Brands that are failing in test market, though expectations were very high.

Businesses whose strengths are being threatened by new competition.

Acquisitions of well-known but poorly performing businesses that need a growth strategy to attain the objectives of the new owners.

 Back to the Turnaround Home Page.

Last updated by Steven Hatch (hatch@turnaround.com) on NOV-01-94

Figure 4.4: The Turnaround Team's brochure (Continued)

Example 5—A large organization's home page

After showing the previous examples of Web pages of individuals and small organizations, I thought this would be a good place to present an example of the home page of a large organization. On October 20, 1994, Vice President Al Gore announced the availability of *The White House World Wide Web Server, An Interactive Citizens' Handbook* at the URL http://www.whitehouse.gov/. This page, which covers the Executive Branch, is at http://www.whitehouse.gov/White_-House/EOP/html/3_parts.html, one jump from the White House home page.

This is a well-designed Web page. All three images on the page have ALT attributes that describe the image for readers with nongraphical browsers, and there is even an alternative text-only page at http://www.whitehouse.gov/White_-House/EOP/html/3_parts-plain.html.

The page begins with an image map. Clicking on this image map will send the cursor coordinates to the script, 3_parts.map, designated in the anchor tags enclosing the image. The script will return a new page depending on the location of the mouse pointer when the reader clicked the mouse button. The page ends with another image map that can take the reader either back to the previous page or to the top of the server. The image file of the Capitol in the middle of the page is referenced with the partial URL ../images/capitol-icon.gif. The double dots should be interpreted to refer to the parent directory of the directory containing the current page.

EXAMPLE 5—A LARGE ORGANIZATION'S HOME PAGE **87**

There's a harmless mistake in the HTML code that will be ignored by all browsers. See if you can find an extra ending anchor tag, </A>.

```
<TITLE>Executive Branch</TITLE>
<!-- Changed by: Miguel Jardine, 15-Oct-1994 -->
<! revised 9/27/94, mjardine>

<A HREF="/imagemap/3_parts.map">
<IMG SRC="/White_House/EOP/images/3_parts.gif" ALT="[Clickable Image]" ISMAP></A>

<P><HR><P>
There are four ways to use this service to look for government information:

<UL>
<LI>By selecting a government agency from one of the categories in the image above.

<LI>By agency using
<A HREF="DC_map.html">a map of Washington, D.C.</A>

<LI>By a
<A HREF="http://www.fedworld.gov/#usgovt">
subject index to government information online</A>,
which is provided by
<A HREF="http://www.fedworld.gov/"> FedWorld</A>.

<LI>By a
<A HREF="http://info.er.usgs.gov/gils/index.html">
government information locator service (GILS)</A>,
which is an index being built to all government information.
</UL>

<P>
<IMG SRC= "../images/capitol-icon.gif" ALT= "[Aerial View of Capitol
Building]"></A>
<A HREF="other_branches.html">
Find Information from Other Branches of the Government</A>

<P><HR>
Choose
<A HREF="/White_House/EOP/html/3_parts-plain.html">this</A>
for a textual representation of this page.

<HR>
<A HREF="/cgi-
bin/previous/0/http://www.whitehouse.gov/White_House/EOP/html/3_parts.html">
<IMG SRC="/White_House/images/bottom_banner.gif" ALT="[W2WH Footer - Clickable
Image]" ISMAP></A>
```

```
<A HREF="/White_House/Keepers/html/Keepers.html">
<ADDRESS>feedback@www.whitehouse.gov</ADDRESS></A>
```

Figure 4.5 shows the Executive Branch page when displayed and printed using NCSA Mosaic.

There are four ways to use this service to look for government information:

By selecting a government agency from one of the categories in the image above.

By agency using a map of Washington, D.C.

By a subject index to government information online, which is provided by FedWorld.

By a government information locator service (GILS), which is an index being built to all government information.

  Find Information from Other Branches of the Government

Choose this for a textual representation of this page.

feedback@www.whitehouse.gov

Figure 4.5: The Executive Branch home page

EXAMPLE 6—A PAGE OF INTERNET RESOURCES **89**

EXAMPLE 6—A PAGE OF INTERNET RESOURCES

A Net friend, Larry Chase, pointed me to the Yahoo Web server at Stanford University, http://akebono.stanford.edu/yahoo/. It's one of the best subject-oriented guides to the Internet, with over 18,000 entries in its database. Three links from the Yahoo home page at URL http://www.rpi.edu/Internet/Guides/-decemj/text.html is this page by John December, entitled *Internet Web Text*. This page is very good HTML. Unlike some of the other examples in this chapter, I've done very little reformatting to make the code more readable.

The page begins with a small transparent gif image followed by a collection of links separated by slashes that provide additional information about the page and alternative versions for nongraphical browsers. The anchors for these links are in italics, aligned with the bottom of the image. The effect is that of a set of buttons across the top of the page. Next, following the first horizontal rule is the page title and authorship information. Note the use of the character entity *ç* to create *Version française.*

```
<HTML>
<HEAD>
    <TITLE>Internet Web Text</TITLE>
    <LINK REV=made HREF="mailto:decemj@rpi.edu">
</HEAD>

<BODY>

<IMG SRC="images/text.gif" ALT="IWT HOME">

<I>
<A HREF="about.html">README</A> /
<A HREF="narrative.html">Narrative</A> /
<A HREF="no-icons.html">No-icons</A> /
<A HREF="compact.html">Compact version</A> /
<A HREF="icons.html">Icons-only</A>
</I>
<BR>

<HR>

<H1>Internet Web Text</H1>

<ADDRESS><A HREF="john_december.html">John December</A>
(decemj@rpi.edu)</ADDRESS>

<A HREF="releases.html">Release </A> 1.20; 22 Sep 1994<BR>
<A HREF="global.html">Global</A> sites:
<A HREF="http://www.rpi.edu/Internet/Guides/decemj/text.html">
```

```
New York, USA</A> / Nancy, France (
<A HREF="http://www.loria.fr/~charoy/InternetWeb/text.html">English</A>,
<A HREF="http://www.loria.fr/~charoy/ToileInternet/text.html">Version
fran&ccedil;aise</A>) /
<A HREF="http://www.unimelb.edu.au:8080/decemj/text.html">
Melbourne, Australia</A>
<BR>
<P>
<HR>
```

After this second horizontal rule begins the main part of the page, beginning with a link to a narrative overview. This entire part of the page is struc-
tured as a series of definition lists with <DL></DL> tags enclosing definition
term <DT> and definition description <DD> tags. Each definition term (except the first) is composed of two anchors, the first enclosing a small square
icon image and the second enclosing a text label. Both point to a single-page
version of the information contained in the definition description paired with
the definition term. The icon points to a graphic version of the page, the label
to a narrative version. The page ends with a short copyright notice using the
character entity *©* for the copyright symbol (©). Some browsers will also
recognize *©* for this symbol.

```
<DL>
<DT><A HREF="narrative.html">Narrative Overview</A>
<P>
<DT><A HREF="orient.html"><IMG SRC="images/page.gif"
    ALT="Orientation List"></A>
    <A HREF="nar-orient.html">Internet Orientation</A>
    <DD>
    <A HREF="ftp://nic.merit.edu/documents/fyi/fyi_20.txt">
    What is the Internet? </A>  *
    <A HREF="ftp://nysernet.org/pub/resources/guides/surfing.2.0.3.txt">
    Surfing the Internet</A>  *
    <A HREF="ftp://ftp.lib.berkeley.edu/pub/net.training/FAU/netiquette.txt">
Netiquette</A>  *
    <A HREF="ftp://ftp.tic.com/matrix/maps/matrix/mat9301.gif">
    Matrix Map</A>  *
    <A HREF="images/cyber.gif">
    CyberMap</A>   *
    <A HREF="http://www.hpcc.gov">
    High Performance Computing and Communications Office (USA)</A>
       *
    (<A HREF="icmc/internet-introduction.html">See also</A>)
</DL>

<DL>
<DT><A HREF="guides.html"><IMG SRC="images/page.gif" ALT="Guides List"></A>
```

EXAMPLE 6—A PAGE OF INTERNET RESOURCES **91**

```
    <A HREF="nar-guides.html">Guides to Using the Internet</A>
    <DD>
    <A HREF="http://www.eff.org/papers/eegtti/eegttitop.html">EFF's Internet
Guide</A>  *
    <A HREF="http://www.earn.net/gnrt/notice.html#contents">EARN's Guide to
Network Resource Tools</A>  *
    <A HREF="http://www.eit.com:80/web/www.guide/"> Entering the World-Wide
Web</A>  *
    <A HREF="http://sundance.cso.uiuc.edu/Publications/Other/Zen/zen-
1.0_toc.html">Zen and the Art of the Internet</A>  *
    <A HREF="http://login.eunet.no/~presno/index.html">The Online World</A>  *
    <A HREF="ftp://mrcnext.cso.uiuc.edu/etext/etext93/email025.txt">Email 101</A> *
    <A HREF="http://alpha.acast.nova.edu/UNIXhelp/TOP_.html">UNIXhelp</A>
       *
    (<A HREF="http://www.rpi.edu/Internet/Guides/decemj/icmc/internet-navigating-
guides.html">See also</A>)
</DL>


<DL>
<DT><A HREF="reference.html"><IMG SRC="images/page.gif" ALT="Reference List"></A>
    <A HREF="nar-reference.html">Internet Reference</A>
    <DD>
    <A HREF="icmc/toc3.html">
    Information Sources </A>  *
    <A HREF="itools/toc3.html">
     Internet Tools</A>  *
    <A HREF="http://www.uwm.edu/Mirror/inet.services.html">
     Special Internet Connections</A>  *
    <A HREF="http://www.internic.net">
     InterNIC</A>  *
    <A HREF="ftp://nic.merit.edu">
     Merit</A>  *
    <A HREF="http://cui_www.unige.ch/OSG/MultimediaInfo/index.html">
     Multimedia Index</A>  *
    <A HREF="ftp://rtfm.mit.edu/pub/usenet/news.answers/internet-services/faq">
     Internet Services FAQ</A>
</DL>


<DL>
<DT><A HREF="browse.html"><IMG SRC="images/page.gif" ALT="Explore List"></A>
    <A HREF="nar-browse.html">Internet Browsing and Exploring</A>
    <DD>
    <A HREF="gopher://gopher.micro.umn.edu:70/1">
    Gopher</A>  *
    <A HREF="http://www.cc.ukans.edu/hytelnet_html/START.TXT.html">
     Hytelnet</A>  *
    <A HREF="http://nearnet.gnn.com/gnn/GNNhome.html">
     Global Network Navigator</A>  *
```

```
    <A HREF="telnet://library.wustl.edu">
     World Window</A>  *
    <A HREF="gopher://gopher.cic.net:70/11/hunt">
     Internet Hunt</A>  *
    <A HREF="icmc/culture.html">
     Cultural Aspects</A>  *
    <A HREF="http://sunsite.unc.edu/expo/ticket_office.html">
     World Wide Web Exhibits</A>
</DL>

<DL>
<DT><A HREF="subject.html"><IMG SRC="images/page.gif"
    ALT="Subjects List"></A>
    <A HREF="nar-subject.html">Subject-Oriented Searching</A>
    <DD>
    <A HREF="http://info.cern.ch./hypertext/DataSources/bySubject/Overview.html">
    WWW Virtual Library</A>  *
    <A HREF="http://www.einet.net/galaxy.html">
     EINet Galaxy</A>  *
    <A HREF="http://akebono.stanford.edu/yahoo/">
     Yahoo </A>  *
    <A HREF="http://www.lib.umich.edu/chhome.html">
     Subject-Oriented Internet Guides</A>  *
    <A HREF="http://galaxy.einet.net/GJ/index.html">
     Gopher Jewels</A>  *
    <A HREF="http://nearnet.gnn.com/wic/newrescat.toc.html">
     O'Reilly's Whole Internet Catalog</A>  *
    <A HREF="http://www.cis.ohio-state.edu/hypertext/faq/usenet/FAQ-List.html">
     USENET Frequently Asked Questions Archive</A>
     *
     (<A HREF="icmc/internet-searching-subjects.html">See also</A>)
</DL>

<DL>
<DT><A HREF="search.html"><IMG SRC="images/page.gif" ALT="Words List"></A>
    <A HREF="nar-search.html">Word-Oriented Searching</A>
    <DD>
    <A HREF="http://cui_www.unige.ch/meta-index.html">
     Web Search</A>
     (<A HREF="http://cui_www.unige.ch/w3catalog">Catalog</A>)
     /
    <A HREF="http://web.nexor.co.uk/susi/susi.html">SUSI</A>
     /
     <A HREF="http://www_is.cs.utwente.nl:8080/cgi-bin/local/nph-susi1.pl">External
info </A>
      *
    <A HREF="http://web.nexor.co.uk/mak/doc/robots/robots.html">
     WWW Wanderers</A>
```

EXAMPLE 6—A PAGE OF INTERNET RESOURCES **93**

```
    (<A HREF="http://fuzine.mt.cs.cmu.edu/cgi-bin/pursuit-test">Lycos</A>,
     <A HREF="http://www.town.hall.org/brokers/www-home-
pages/query.html">Harvest</A>,
       <A HREF="http://www.biotech.washington.edu/WebQuery.html">Crawler</A>)
        *
    <A HREF="http://galaxy.einet.net/gopher/gopher.html">
     Gopher Jewels Search</A>  *
     <A HREF="gopher://gopher.nd.edu/11/Non-
Notre%20Dame%20Information%20Sources/Phone%20Books--Other%20Institutions">
     Directory Services</A>  *
     <A HREF="telnet://info.cnri.reston.va.us:185">
     Knowbot</A>  *
     <A HREF="http://info.cern.ch/hypertext/DataSources/WWW/Servers.html">
     World-Wide Web Servers</A>  *
     <A HREF="http://web.nexor.co.uk/archie.html">ArchiePlexForm</A>
        *
     (See also: <A HREF="icmc/internet-searching-keyword.html">keywords</A>,
       <A HREF="icmc/internet-searching-people.html">people</A>)
</DL>


<DL>
<DT><A HREF="people.html"><IMG SRC="images/page.gif" ALT="People List"></A>
     <A HREF="nar-people.html">Connecting with People</A>
     <DD>
     <A HREF="wais://munin.ub2.lu.se:210/academic_email_conf">
     Academic Discussion Lists</A>  *
     <A HREF="http://alpha.acast.nova.edu/cgi-bin/lists">
      General Discussion Lists</A>  *
     <A HREF="http://info.cern.ch/hypertext/DataSources/News/Groups/Overview.html">
      Usenet Newsgroups</A>  *
     <A HREF="http://www.kei.com/irc.html">
      Internet Relay Chat</A>  *
     <A HREF="http://www.cis.upenn.edu/~lwl/mudinfo.html">
      Multiple User Dialogues</A> *
     <A HREF="icmc/culture-people-lists.html">
      People Lists (directories, home pages)</A> *
     (<A HREF="itools/cmc.html">See also: CMC Forums</A>)
</DL>


<HR>

<A HREF="copyright.html">Copyright &#169; 1994 John December</A>

</BODY>
</HTML>
```

Figure 4.6 shows how the Internet Web Text page generated by this HTML code will appear when displayed and printed using NCSA Mosaic.

Internet Web Text README / _Narrative_ / _No-icons_ / _Compact version_ / _Icons-only_

Internet Web Text

John December (decemj@rpi.edu)
Release 1.20; 22 Sep 1994
Global sites: New York, USA / Nancy, France (English, Version française) / Melbourne, Australia

Narrative Overview

Internet Orientation
What is the Internet? * Surfing the Internet * Netiquette * Matrix Map * CyberMap * High Performance Computing and Communications Office (USA) * (See also)

Guides to Using the Internet
EFF's Internet Guide * EARN's Guide to Network Resource Tools * Entering the World-Wide Web * Zen and the Art of the Internet * The Online World * Email 101 * UNIXhelp * (See also)

Internet Reference
Information Sources * Internet Tools * Special Internet Connections * InterNIC * Merit * Multimedia Index * Internet Services FAQ

Internet Browsing and Exploring
Gopher * Hytelnet * Global Network Navigator * World Window * Internet Hunt * Cultural Aspects * World Wide Web Exhibits

Subject-Oriented Searching
WWW Virtual Library * EINet Galaxy * Yahoo * Subject-Oriented Internet Guides * Gopher Jewels * O'Reilly's Whole Internet Catalog * USENET Frequently Asked Questions Archive * (See also)

Word-Oriented Searching

Figure 4.6: The Internet Web Text home page

EXAMPLE 7—A PAGE COVERING A SUBJECT FIELD   **95**

Web Search (Catalog) / SUSI / External info * WWW Wanderers (Lycos, Harvest, Crawler) * Gopher Jewels Search * Directory Services * Knowbot * World-Wide Web Servers * ArchiePlexForm * (See also: keywords, people)

Connecting with People
Academic Discussion Lists * General Discussion Lists * Usenet Newsgroups * Internet Relay Chat * Multiple User Dialogues * People Lists (directories, home pages) * (See also: CMC Forums)

Copyright ©1994 John December

Figure 4.6: The Internet Web Text home page (Continued)

EXAMPLE 7—A PAGE COVERING A SUBJECT FIELD

This is one of my favorite pages on the Web. I met Dr. Godwin-Jones at the Second International World Wide Web Conference, where his Web work was presented in a poster session. I love languages, both natural and artificial. (I wish there was something on this page about Lingala; unfortunately, the parts of the world where this beautiful language is spoken don't even have e-mail.) The other reason this page is one of my favorites is the clever use of transparent gif images.

The HTML code begins with a page header identifying the site and provides links to other Web servers at Virginia Commonwealth University. Following this, under the heading *Scenic Side Trails,* is a definition list with four links. Although using a definition list in this manner—definition terms without matching definition descriptions—is not strictly good HTML usage, it is a technique used by many authors to provide a slight indent to a block of text. It seems to work, at least with the four graphical browsers I have at my disposal. If you choose this technique, use it with care.

```
<HTML>
<HEAD>
<TITLE> International Guide</TITLE>
</HEAD>

<BODY>
<IMG SRC = "trail.gif" ALT= "VCU INTERNATIONAL TRAIL GUIDE"><BR>
```

```
<A HREF="http://cabell.vcu.edu/vcu/vcuhome.html">
Virginia Commonwealth University</A> -
<A HREF = http://opal.vcu.edu>VIEWS</A> -
<A HREF="Dept.html">Foreign Language Department</A> <BR>

<H3><IMG ALIGN=bottom SRC = "hiker.gif">Scenic Side Trails</H3>

<DL>
<DT> <A HREF="http://mistral.enst.fr/~pioch/louvre/paintings/">
Le Louvre</A>  English/French: see  impressionists, Picasso, etc.

<DT> <A HREF= "http://itre.uncecs.edu/music/cuban-music.html">
Cuban Music</A>  English/Spanish:  hear some sound samples

<DT> <A HREF= "http://imtsun3.epfl.ch:8000/tango//welcome.html">
Tangofolie</A>  English:  videos; learn how Arnold did those steps

<DT> <A HREF = "menu.html">German stories</A>
German/English:  multimedia editions (from VCU)
</DL>
```

The next section, beginning with the heading *International Sites by Map,* contains another definition list to provide indentation. Within that definition list is a set of nested unordered lists, some of which contain only a single entry. Perhaps there will be more entries later. I've indented the HTML code to match the list nesting for easier reading.

```
<H3><IMG ALIGN=bottom SRC="compass.gif">International Sites by Map</H3>

[A text
<A HREF="http://info.cern.ch/hypertext/DataSources/WWW/Servers.html"> summary</A>
and a
<A HREF="http://info.cern.ch/hypertext/DataSources/WWW/Geographical.html">
full</A> alphabetical list are also available]
<P>
<DL>
  <UL>
    <LI><A HREF="http://wings.buffalo.edu/world/">World</A>
    <UL>
      <LI><A HREF="http://s700.uminho.pt/europa.html">Europe</A>
      <UL>
        <LI><A HREF="http://web.urec.fr/france/france.html">France</A>
        <UL>
          <LI><A HREF="http://mistral.enst.fr/~pioch/louvre/paris/">
              Paris</A>
        </UL>
```

Example 7—A page covering a subject field   **97**

```
        <LI><A HREF="http://www.informatik.tu-
            muenchen.de/isar/WWWother/demap.html">Germany</A>
        <UL>
          <LI><A HREF= "http://httpserver.forwiss.uni-
              passau.de/passau/stadt/plan/uebersicht.html"> Passau</A>
        </UL>
        <LI> <A HREF="http://www.mi.cnr.it/NIR-IT/NIR-
            map.html">Italy</A>
        <UL>
          <LI><A HREF= "http://www.unipr.it/">Parma</A>
        </UL>
        <LI>Russia
        <UL>
          <LI>Moscow
          <UL>
            <LI><A HREF="http://www.kiae.su/www/wtr/kremlin/begin.html">
                The Kremlin</A>
          </UL>
        </UL>
        <LI> <A HREF="http://www.uji.es/spain_www.html">Spain</A>
      </UL>
      <LI>Asia
      <UL>
        <LI><A HREF="http://www.ntt.jp/AP/asia-NE.html">Japan</A>
      </UL>
    </UL>
  </UL>
</DL>
```

This next section under the heading *International Information,* starts with a couple of paragraphs, the second of which is a string of links to various countries. Following that is a simple unordered list.

```
<H3><IMG ALIGN=bottom SRC="globei.gif">International Information</H3>

<EM>INFORMATION BY COUNTRY</EM><BR>
These sites are often very informative, both on the country and on related
Internet resources. For countries not listed, consult this
<A HREF= "http://nearnet.gnn.com/gnn/meta/travel/cglist.html">
source</A>.  If you're planing to go abroad,  get <A HREF= "http://www.ora.com/cgi-
bin/ora/currency">currency</A> information.
<p>
<A HREF= "http://www.ar:70/">Argentina</A> -
<A HREF= "http://pespmc1.vub.ac.be/Belgcul.html">Belgium</A> -
<A HREF= "http://guarani.cos.ufrj.br:8000/Rio/Todas.html">Brazil</A> -
<A HREF= "http://pisa.rockefeller.edu:8080/Bulgaria/">Bulgaria</A> -
```

```
<A HREF= "http://www.dcc.uchile.cl/chile/chile.html">Chile </A> -
<A HREF="http://ftp.netcom.com/pub/ducky/docs/france/france.html">
France</A> -
<A HREF="http://www.chemie.fu-berlin.de/adressen/brd.html">Germany</A> -
<A HREF= "http://www.lib.klte.hu/index.english.html">Hungary</A> -
<A HREF= "http://www.rhi.hi.is/HIHome.html">Iceland</A> -
<A HREF= "http://www.umanitoba.ca/indonesian/homepage.html">
Indonesia</A> -
<A HREF="http://itdsrv1.ul.ie/Information/Ireland.html">Ireland</A> -
<A HREF="http://www.mi.cnr.it/NIR-IT/Italy.html">Italy</A> -
<A HREF="http://fuji.stanford.edu/japan_information/japan_information_guide.html">
Japan</A> -
<A HREF= "http://www.rcp.net.pe/peru/peru.html">Peru </A> -
<A HREF= "http://osprey.unisa.ac.za/0/docs/south-africa.html">
South Africa</A> -
<A HREF= "http://www.umiacs.umd.edu/research/lpv/YU/HTML/yu.html">
Yugoslavia</A> (Serbia/Montenegro)<p>

<EM>INTERNATIONAL STUDIES</EM>
<UL>
<LI> <A HREF= "http://coombs.anu.edu.au/WWWVL-AsianStudies.html">
Asian Studies </A>
<LI><A HREF="http://lanic.utexas.edu/las.html">
Latin American Studies</A> (indices to 11 countries)
<LI> <A HREF= "http://www.pitt.edu/~cjp/rees.html">
Russian and East European Studies</A> (excellent; info on Russian Web servers)
<LI> <A HREF= "http://www.georgetown.edu/labyrinth/labyrinth-home.html">
Medieval Studies</A> (Labyrinth project at Georgetown University)
</UL>
<P>
```

This next section, *Where to Pitch Your Tent*, uses another definition list to order a set of links. Note the use of character entities to properly render French and German names containing non-ASCII characters.

```
<H3><IMG SRC="tent.gif">Where to Pitch Your Tent</H3>
[Most sites have (at least some) information in English]

<DL>
<DT> Brazil <A HREF = "http://www.inf.ufsc.br">
University of Santa Catarina</A> - VCU partner university
<DT> France <A HREF= "http://www.univ-pau.fr/">
Universit&eacute; de Pau </A> -  VCU partner university
<DT> Germany <A HREF= "http://www.fmi.uni-passau.de/welcome.html">Universit&auml;t
Passau </A>
  -  One of the better German sites
```

Example 7—A page covering a subject field **99**

```
<DT> Indonesia <A HREF= "http://www.umanitoba.ca/indonesian/persons.html">
Manusia Indonesia</A> - Meet Indonesians one on one
<DT> Russia <A HREF= "http://www.kiae.su/www/wtr/">Window-to-Russia</A> - Good
summary of Russian Internet resources
</DL>
```

This next large section under the heading *Campfire Reading* is a series of un-ordered lists, one per language, with a level 4 heading introducing each. Note that the first list item under the heading *French* is a gopher server—the English-Server at Carnegie Melon University. The URL for the gopher uses special escape sequences (percent signs [%] followed by two hexadecimal characters) for separators in the directory path. This is not necessary; the URL was probably copied from another source. Also note the use of the TITLE attribute in the anchor for the gopher to provide the browser with information that would normally be missing from a non-Web server.

```
<H3><IMG ALIGN=bottom SRC="campfire.gif" >
Campfire Reading: Language Resources and Texts
</H3>

<H4>Arabic</H4>
<UL>
<LI> <A HREF= "http://philae.sas.upenn.edu/Arabic/arabic.html">
Let's Learn Arabic</A> (includes audio, video)
<LI> <A HREF="gopher://gopher.ncsu.edu/00/ref_desk/sacred/quran/quran-dict"
TITLE=Dictionary>Dictionary of Qur'anic Arabic</A> (in word list form)
</UL>

<H4> Chinese</H4>
<UL>
<LI><A HREF= "http://nearnet.gnn.com/wic/lit.15.html">
Chinese Literature</A> (novels, poetry and classics; FTP)
<LI><A HREF= "ftp://ftp.netcom/pub/mcevilly/www/chinfo.html">
Chinese language-related info</A>
</UL>

<H4>French</H4>
<UL>
<LI><A HREF="gopher://english-
server.hss.cmu.edu/11ftp%3aEnglish%20Server%3aLanguage%3aFrench%20Flash%20Cards%3a"
 TITLE=French>French Flash Cards</A> (gopher)
<LI><A HREF= "http://cuisg13.unige.ch:8100/franco.html"> Le coin des francophones
et autres grenouilles</A> (general info on French resources)
<LI> <A HREF= "http://tuna.uchicago.edu/images/heures/heures.html"> Les
tr&egrave;s riches heures du duc du Berry</A> (includes images)
```

```
 <LI><A HREF= "http://www.lib.virginia.edu/etext/french.html">French texts</A>
(from U.of Virginia:  from medieval to modern; information)
<LI><A HREF= "http://tuna.uchicago.edu:/ARTFL.html">French Literature
Collection</A> (ARTFL Project at the U.of Chicago; information)
</UL>

<H4>German</H4>
<UL>
<LI> <A HREF="http://www.fmi.uni-passau.de/htbin/lt/lte">
English-German Dictionary</A> (interactive)
<LI> <A HREF="http://www.fmi.uni-passau.de/htbin/lt/ltd">
German-English Dictionary</A> (interactive)
<LI> <A HREF= "gopher://alpha.epas.utoronto.ca/11/cch/disciplines/german">
German Language Resources</A> (gopher)
<LI><A HREF= "menu.html">19th-Century Stories</A>
(Struwwelpeter, Busch, Grimm Bros.; hypertext)
<LI><A
HREF="gopher://gopher.epas.utoronto.ca/11/cch/disciplines/german/texts/ids">German
Literature searchable corpus</A> (Goethe, Thomas Mann, Marx; telnet)
</UL>

<H4>Italian</H4>
<UL>
<LI><A HREF= "http://www.crs4.it/HTML/Literature.html">
Italian literature</A> (from Divine Comedy (selections) to Pinocchio; hypertext)
<LI> <A HREF= "gopher://gopher.dartmouth.edu/1/AnonFTP/pub/Dante">
Dante Project</A> (collects 600 years of Dante commentary; gopher)
<LI><A HREF= "http://www.crs4.it/~ruggiero/unione.html">
"L'Unione Sarda" on-line</A> (Italian; hypertext)
</UL>

<H4>Japanese</H4>
<UL>
<LI> <A HREF="http://www.ntt.jp/japan/japanese/">
Traveler's Japanese</A> (audio)
<LI> <A HREF="gopher://english-
server.hss.cmu.edu/00ftp%3aEnglish%20Server%3aLanguage%3aQuick%20%26%20Dirty%20
Japanese" TITLE=Quick>Quick & Dirty Japanese</A> (gopher)
</UL>

<H4>Latin</H4>
<UL>
<LI> <A HREF="gopher://wiretap.spies.com/00/Library/Article/Language/latin.stu"
TITLE=Study>Study Guide to Wheelock Latin</A> (text)
</UL>
```

Example 7—A page covering a subject field   **101**

```
<H4>Russian</H4>
<UL>
<LI> <A HREF="http://sunsite.oit.unc.edu/sergei/Grandsons.html">Dazhdbog's
Grandsons</A>  (info on how to handle cyrillic on the Internet)
<LI><A HREF="http://solar.rtd.utk.edu/friends/home.html">
Friends and Parners</A> (more on cyrillic on the Internet)
<LI> <A HREF="gopher://english-
server.hss.cmu.edu/11ftp%3aEnglish%20Server%3aLanguage%3aRussian%3a"
TITLE=Russian>Russian</A> (gopher)
</UL>

<H4> Swedish</H4>
<UL>
<LI><A HREF= "http://www.lysator.liu.se:7500/bw/runeberg/Main.html">
Project Runeberg Scandinavian texts</A> (Swedish and Finnish; FTP)
</UL>

<H4>Welsh</H4>
<UL>
<LI> <A HREF= "http://www.cs.brown.edu/fun/welsh/home.html">
A Welsh Course</A> (for beginners; also listing of resources on Welsh; hypertext)
</UL>

<H3>
<IMG ALIGN=bottom SRC="lamp.gif" >Other Language Learning Resources
</H3>
<UL>
<LI>Review of <A HREF = "fllists2.html">
Internet/Bitnet discussion groups</A> for language learning
<LI>Schedule for <A HREF ="gopher://bluejay.creighton.edu/11/aux/scola/schedule">
SCOLA</A> satellite foreign language broadcasts
</UL>

<HR>
<ADDRESS>
<A HREF = gj.html><b>rgjones</b></A>@cabell.vcu.edu
<P>
Last Update: 9/18/94
</ADDRESS>
```

Figure 4.7 shows the final VCU Trail Guide page generated by this HTML code as it appears when displayed and printed using NCSA Mosaic.

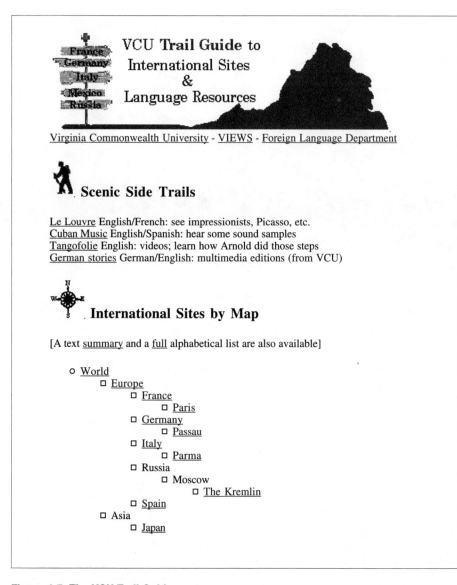

Figure 4.7: The VCU Trail Guide page

EXAMPLE 7—A PAGE COVERING A SUBJECT FIELD **103**

International Information

INFORMATION BY COUNTRY
These sites are often very informative, both on the country and on related Internet resources. For countries not listed, consult this <u>source</u>. If you're planing to go abroad get <u>currency</u> information.

<u>Argentina</u> - <u>Belgium</u> - <u>Brazil</u> - <u>Bulgaria</u> - <u>Chile</u> - <u>France</u> - <u>Germany</u> - <u>Hungary</u> - <u>Iceland</u> - <u>Indonesia</u> - <u>Ireland</u> - <u>Italy</u> - <u>Japan</u> - <u>Peru</u> - <u>South Africa</u> - <u>Yugoslavia</u> (Serbia/Montenegro)

INTERNATIONAL STUDIES

- <u>Asian Studies</u>
- <u>Latin American Studies</u> (indices to 11 countries)
- <u>Russian and East European Studies</u> (excellent; info on Russian Web servers)
- <u>Medieval Studies</u> (Labyrinth project at Georgetown University)

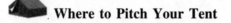 **Where to Pitch Your Tent**

[Most sites have (at least some) information in English]

Brazil <u>University of Santa Catarina</u> - VCU partner university
France <u>Université de Pau</u> - VCU partner university
Germany <u>Universität Passau</u> - One of the better German sites
Indonesia <u>Manusia Indonesia</u> - Meet Indonesians one on one
Russia <u>Window-to-Russia</u> - Good summary of Russian Internet resources

Campfire Reading: Language Resources and Texts

Arabic

- <u>Let's Learn Arabic</u> (includes audio, video)
- <u>Dictionary of Qur'anic Arabic</u> (in word list form)

Figure 4.7: The VCU Trail Guide page (Continued)

Chinese

- Chinese Literature (novels, poetry and classics; FTP)
- Chinese language-related info

French

- French Flash Cards (gopher)
- Le coin des francophones et autres grenouilles (general info on French resources)
- Les très riches heures du duc du Berry (includes images)
- French texts (from U.of Virginia: from medieval to modern; information)
- French Literature Collection (ARTFL Project at the U.of Chicago; information)

German

- English-German Dictionary (interactive)
- German-English Dictionary (interactive)
- German Language Resources (gopher)
- 19th-Century Stories (Struwwelpeter, Busch, Grimm Bros.; hypertext)
- German Literature searchable corpus (Goethe, Thomas Mann, Marx; telnet)

Italian

- Italian literature (from Divine Comedy (selections) to Pinocchio; hypertext)
- Dante Project (collects 600 years of Dante commentary; gopher)
- "L'Unione Sarda" on-line (Italian; hypertext)

Japanese

- Traveler's Japanese (audio)
- Quick & Dirty Japanese (gopher)

Latin

- Study Guide to Wheelock Latin (text)

Figure 4.7: The VCU Trail Guide page (Continued)

EXAMPLE 8—ANOTHER HOME PAGE   **105**

Russian

- Dazhdbog's Grandsons (info on how to handle cyrillic on the Internet)
- Friends and Parners (more on cyrillic on the Internet)
- Russian (gopher)

Swedish

- Project Runeberg Scandinavian texts (Swedish and Finnish; FTP)

Welsh

- A Welsh Course (for beginners; also listing of resources on Welsh; hypertext

Other Language Learning Resources

- Review of Internet/Bitnet discussion groups for language learning
- Schedule for SCOLA satellite foreign language broadcasts

rgjones @cabell.vcu.edu

Last Update: 9/18/94

Figure 4.7: The VCU Trail Guide page (Continued)

EXAMPLE 8—ANOTHER HOME PAGE

This last example is one of the best HTML works I've found on the Web, which comes as no surprise as it is the home page of BayCHI, The Bay Area chapter of the Association for Computing Machinery's (ACM's) special interest group on computer-human interaction. What makes this page so good is that it's short, reader friendly, and it makes excellent use of graphics. The only way I feel it can be improved is by removing the extra paragraph tags and by adding authorship and date information on the bottom. The URL for the page is http://info.acm.org/~BayCHI/homepage.html.

```
<HTML>
<HEAD>
<TITLE>BayCHI</TITLE>
</HEAD>
```

```
<BODY>
<IMG SRC="graphics/baychi.gif">
<P>
<H1>Welcome to BayCHI</H1>
<IMG SRC="graphics/workers.gif">
<P>
<STRONG>These web pages are still under construction. Please excuse the unfinished
look and incomplete state.</STRONG>
<P>
BayCHI is the San Francisco Bay Area chapter of ACM's Special Interest Group on
Computer-Human Interaction.
<P>
<HR>
<STRONG><A HREF="meetings/baychi_meetings.html">
October Meeting</A> - Tuesday, October 11, 1994</STRONG>

<H2>
Too Much Hypertext or Too Little?
<ADDRESS>Jakob Nielsen, SunSoft</ADDRESS>
</H2>
<HR>
<P>
<A HREF="general/baychi_general.html">
<IMG SRC="graphics/baychi-info.gif" ALIGN=middle>BayCHI</A>
<P>
<A HREF="meetings/baychi_meetings.html">
<IMG SRC="graphics/meetings.gif" ALIGN=middle>Meetings</A>
<P>
<A HREF="calendar/baychi_calendar.html">
<IMG SRC="graphics/calendar.gif" ALIGN=middle>Calendar</a>
<P>
<P>
<ADDRESS>
If you have any problems with this service, please contact baychi@acm.org
<P>
</ADDRESS>
</BODY>
</HTML>
```

Figure 4.8 shows the BayCHI page as it appears on the screen.

I hope these examples have helped you to understand how you can use HTML for your applications. If you've found any of these particularly interesting, why not create a hotlist or bookmark entry for it in your browser so you can revisit it later and see if it has changed?

EXAMPLE 8—ANOTHER HOME PAGE **107**

Welcome to BayCHI

These web pages are still under construction. Please excuse the unfinished look and incomplete state.

BayCHI is the San Francisco Bay Area chapter of ACM's Special Interest Group on Computer-Human Interaction.

October Meeting - Tuesday, October 11, 1994

Too Much Hypertext or Too Little?

Jakob Nielsen, SunSoft

 BayCHI

 Meetings

Calendar

If you have any problems with this service, please contact baychi@acm.org

Figure 4.8: The BayCHI page

APPENDIX A:
HTML QUICK REFERENCE

The alphabetical listing of HTML markup elements shown in Table A.1 is taken from the HTML 2.0 DTD specification. It should not be considered either definitive or 100 percent complete, but rather, a compact guide to the most useful and commonly found features of Hypertext Markup Language. The reader is referred to the online HTML documentation (see Appendix C) for a complete description.

The presentation of each markup element includes the syntax of the tag, a short description, the attributes that can be specified with the tag, and the context in which the tag may appear. The syntax description takes one of two forms: <IMG>, for example, indicates an empty tag; <H1>...</H1> indicates a nonempty tag enclosing some portion of the document's contents, either text or an image or both.

Attributes take one of two forms: either *ATTRIBUTE="value"*, where *value* is some text enclosed in quotes; or just simply *ATTRIBUTE* without a value. In the description below, *value* may take one of the following forms:

URL	The value is a Uniform Resource Locator.
name	The value is a name supplied by the user, typically to identify an input field.
number	The value is a number supplied by the user.
text	The value is text supplied by the user.
[A I B I ...]	The value is one from a fixed set of values, A, B, ...

Table A.1: HTML Markup Elements

Tag	Description	Attributes	Context
<A>...</A>	Anchor. Marks either the origin or the destination of a link.	HREF="URL" NAME="text" REL=["next" | "previous" | "parent" | "made"] REV="next" | "previous" | "parent" | "made"] TITLE="text"	<ADDRESS> <B> <CITE> <CODE> <DD> <DT> <EM> <H1> <H2> <H3> <H4> <H5> <H6> <I> <KBD> <LI> <PRE> <SAMP> <STRONG> <TT> <VAR>
<ADDRESS>... </ADDRESS>	Address style. Used for addresses, signatures, authorship information, and so on		<BLOCKQUOTE> <BODY> <FORM>
<B>...</B>	Bold style		{Same as anchor}
<BASE>	Base. Used to provide a reference to resolve relative addressing.	HREF="URL"	<HEAD>
<BLOCKQUOTE>... </BLOCKQUOTE>	Used for material quoted from an external source		<BLOCKQUOTE> <BODY> <DD> <FORM> <LI>
<BODY>... </BODY>	Designates the content of an HTML document as opposed to the document's heading		<HTML>
 	Line break. Used to start a new line within a paragraph		{Same as anchor}
<CITE>...</CITE>	Citation style. Used for titles of other works.		{Same as anchor}

Table A.1: HTML Markup Elements (Continued)

Tag	Description	Attributes	Context
<CODE>...</CODE>	Coding style. Used for samples of computer programs.		{Same as anchor}
<DD>	Definition description. The description part of a definition list item.		<DL> {Paired with <DT>}
<DIR>...</DIR>	Directory list. Used for lists typically containing short items such as file names.		<BLOCKQUOTE> <BODY> <DD> <FORM> <LI>
<DL>...</DL>	Definition list. Used for glossaries.		<BLOCKQUOTE> <BODY> <DD> <FORM> <LI>
<DT>	Definition term. The label part of a definition list item.		<DL> {Paired with <DD>}
<EM>...</EM>	Emphasis, typically underlining, to bring out the text from the background		{Same as anchor}
<FORM>...</FORM>	Input form. For defining an area on the page to contain objects for input from the reader.	ACTION="URL" METHOD=["GET" | "POST"]	<BLOCKQUOTE> <BODY> <DD> <LI>
<H1>...</H1>	Level 1 heading		<BLOCKQUOTE> <BODY> <FORM>
<H2>...</H2>	Level 2 heading		<BLOCKQUOTE> <BODY> <FORM>
<H3>...</H3>	Level 3 heading		<BLOCKQUOTE> <BODY> <FORM>
<H4>...</H4>	Level 4 heading		<BLOCKQUOTE> <BODY> <FORM>

Table A.1: HTML Markup Elements (Continued)

Tag	Description	Attributes	Context
<H5>...</H5>	Level 5 heading		<BLOCKQUOTE> <BODY> <FORM>
<H6>...</H6>	Level 6 heading		<BLOCKQUOTE> <BODY> <FORM>
<HEAD>...</HEAD>	Head. Defines that part of the document containing information about the page.		<HTML>
<HR>	Horizontal rule. Draws a line across the width of the page.		<BLOCKQUOTE> <BODY> <FORM> <PRE>
<HTML>...</HTML>	Defines the contents to be of the HTML doctype. Optional with most browsers.		
<I>...</I>	Italics style		{Same as anchor}
<IMG>	Image. Used to place an in-line image into the page.	SRC="URL" ALT="text" ALIGN=["TOP" | "MIDDLE" | "BOT-TOM"] ISMAP	{Same as anchor}
<INPUT>	Defines an input object in a form	TYPE=["TEXT" | "CHECKBOX" | "RADIO" | "SUBMIT" | "RESET"] NAME="name" VALUE="text" SIZE="number" MAXLENGTH= "number" CHECKED	<FORM>
<ISINDEX>	Indicates that a searchable index for the document is avail-able on the server		<HEAD>

Table A.1: HTML Markup Elements (Continued)

Tag	Description	Attributes	Context
<KBD>...</KBD>	Keyboard style for text to be typed into a computer		{Same as anchor}
<LI>	List item		<DIR> <MENU> <OL> <UL>
<LINK>	Provides information relating the current document to other documents or entities	HREF="URL" TITLE="text" REL=["next" | "previous" | "parent" | "made"] REV=["next" | "previous" | "parent" | "made"]	<HEAD>
<MENU>... </MENU>	Menu list		<BLOCKQUOTE> <BODY> <DD> <FORM> <LI>
<OL>...</OL>	Ordered list		<BLOCKQUOTE> <BODY> <DD> <FORM> <LI>
<OPTION>	Defines an item for a SELECT input object	VALUE="text" SELECTED	<SELECT>
<P>	Paragraph break		<BLOCKQUOTE> <BODY> <DD> <FORM> <LI>
<PRE>...</PRE>	Preformatted style	WIDTH="number"	<BLOCKQUOTE> <BODY> <DD> <FORM> <LI>
<SAMP>...</SAMP>	Sample style. Used for examples.		{Same as anchor}
<SELECT>... </SELECT>	Selection input object	NAME="name" SIZE="number" MULTIPLE	<FORM>

Table A.1: HTML Markup Elements (Continued)

Tag	Description	Attributes	Context
<STRONG>...</STRONG>	Strong emphasis style		{Same as anchor}
<TEXTAREA >...</TEXTAREA>	Multiline input object	NAME="name" ROWS="number" COLS="number"	<FORM>
<TITLE>...</TITLE>	Document title		<HEAD>
<TT>...</TT>	Typewriter style (i.e. a monospaced font)		{Same as anchor}
<UL>...</UL>	Unordered list	COMPACT	<BLOCKQUOTE> <BODY> <DD> <FORM> <LI>
<VAR>...</VAR>	Variable style. For names to be supplied by reader.		{Same as anchor}

The following HTML character entities are always prefixed by an ampersand (&) and followed by a semicolon as shown. They represent particular graphic characters that have special meanings in the markup, or that may not be part of the character set available to the HTML writer.

&lt   Less-than sign (<)

&gt   Greater-than sign (>)

&   Ampersand (&)

"   Double quote (")

        Nonbreaking space

Also defined are the following references to any of the ISO Latin-1 alphabet, using the entity names below.

Æ   Uppercase AE diphthong (ligature)

Á   Uppercase A, acute accent

Â   Uppercase A, circumflex accent

&Agrave;	Uppercase A, grave accent
&Aring;	Uppercase A, ring
&Atilde	Uppercase A, tilde
&Auml;	Uppercase A, dieresis or umlaut mark
&Ccedil;	Uppercase C, cedilla
&ETH;	Uppercase Eth, Icelandic
&Eacute;	Uppercase E, acute accent
&Ecirc;	Uppercase E, circumflex accent
&Egrave;	Uppercase E, grave accent
&Euml;	Uppercase E, dieresis or umlaut mark
&Iacute;	Uppercase I, acute accent
&Icirc;	Uppercase I, circumflex accent
&Igrave;	Uppercase I, grave accent
&Iuml;	Uppercase I, dieresis or umlaut mark
&Ntilde;	Uppercase N, tilde
&Oacute;	Uppercase O, acute accent
&Ocirc;	Uppercase O, circumflex accent
&Ograve;	Uppercase O, grave accent
&Oslash;	Uppercase O, slash
&Otilde;	Uppercase O, tilde
&Ouml;	Uppercase O, dieresis or umlaut mark
&THORN;	Uppercase THORN, Icelandic
&Uacute;	Uppercase U, acute accent
&Ucirc;	Uppercase U, circumflex accent
&Ugrave;	Uppercase U, grave accent
&Uuml;	Uppercase U, dieresis or umlaut mark
&Yacute;	Uppercase Y, acute accent
&aacute;	Lowercase a, acute accent
&acirc;	Lowercase a, circumflex accent
&aelig;	Lowercase ae diphthong (ligature)

&agrave;	Lowercase a, grave accent
&aring;	Lowercase a, ring
&atilde;	Lowercase a, tilde
&auml;	Lowercase a, dieresis or umlaut mark
&ccedil;	Lowercase c, cedilla
&eacute;	Lowercase e, acute accent
&ecirc;	Lowercase e, circumflex accent
&egrave;	Lowercase e, grave accent
&eth;	Lowercase eth, Icelandic
&euml;	Lowercase e, dieresis or umlaut mark
&iacute;	Lowercase i, acute accent
&icirc;	Lowercase i, circumflex accent
&igrave;	Lowercase i, grave accent
&iuml;	Lowercase i, dieresis or umlaut mark
&ntilde;	Lowercase n, tilde
&oacute;	Lowercase o, acute accent
&ocirc;	Lowercase o, circumflex accent
&ograve;	Lowercase o, grave accent
&oslash;	Lowercase o, slash
&otilde;	Lowercase o, tilde
&ouml;	Lowercase o, dieresis or umlaut mark
&szlig;	Lowercase sharp s, German (sz ligature)
&thorn;	Lowercase thorn, Icelandic
&uacute;	Lowercase u, acute accent
&ucirc;	Lowercase u, circumflex accent
&ugrave;	Lowercase u, grave accent
&uuml;	Lowercase u, dieresis or umlaut mark
&yacute;	Lowercase y, acute accent
&yuml;	Lowercase y, dieresis or umlaut mark

Appendix B:
HTML+ Overview

Versions of Hypertext Markup Language beyond the level 2 specification are collectively referred to as HTML+. The significant additions to the HTML DTD are new markup tags for figures and tables, plus many new attributes for the existing elements. This appendix provides a brief overview of these new features for the purpose of planning new World Wide Web documents. Authors are free to include some of these elements in current works. Even though most browsers do not currently offer support for these features, most browsers will safely ignore them.

There was a flurry of activity within the HTML discussion groups in late 1993 regarding the future of HTML. A draft document on the subject was produced, which can be found at http://info.cern.ch/hypertext/WWW/MarkUp/HTML-Plus/htmlplus_1.html. This document has since expired. However, the discussions on HTML+ continue, spurred on by the availability of new graphical browsers, each introducing a slightly different set of language extensions. It's not possible to list everybody's language extensions; therefore, this description centers on the HTML+ draft as the common basis for these versions. At this writing, Netscape, an advanced Web browser from Netscape Communications (http://www.mcom.com/), is generating a lot of excitement. Netscape's HTML extensions depart significantly from the HTML+ draft. I've described them separately at the end of this appendix.

In HTML+, most nonempty markup tags, including the paragraph tag, can take the LANG and ID attributes. The LANG attribute is used to specify that a language other than the default ISO-Latin 1 alphabet should be used for the marked-up text. The ISO defines abbreviations for most of the common languages, such as

FR for French. The ID attribute can be used to assign a name to the marked-up text as an alternative to using an anchor with the NAME attribute. For example:

```
<H2 ID="Tagalog_intro">Introduction to Tagalog</H2>
```

can be used in place of

```
<H2><A NAME="Tagalog_intro">Introduction to Tagalog</A></H2>
```

In addition to the ID and LANG attributes, the paragraph tag has an ALIGN tag that can take the left, right, justify, and indent values, as well as a WRAP attribute that, when given the value "off", will disable line wrapping for the extent of the paragraph. With WRAP="off", line breaks must be used to explicitly control the text. An additional method of specifying line breaks is provided with the <L> tag, which, unlike <BR>, can take an ID attribute to designate the destination of a hypertext link. In contrast to HTML 2.0, the HTML+ paragraph tag, <P>, is regarded as nonempty and the use of a closing tag, </P>, is encouraged (though not required); older documents will continue to work correctly without closing paragraph tags.

HTML+ has these additional style tags:

<ABBREV>...</ABBREV>	Abbreviations
<ACRONYM>...</ACRONYM>	Acronyms
<ARG>...</ARG>	Command argument, such as <ARG>-a</ARG>
<CMD>...</CMD>	Command name, such as <CMD>ls</CMD> in Unix
<DFN>...</DFN>	Defining instance of a term
<LIT>...</LIT>	Literal: Like <PRE> but using a proportional font
<PERSON>...</PERSON>	Proper names, such as <PERSON>Nikola Tesla</PERSON>
<Q>...</Q>	A short quotation that can be included in line
<S>...</S>	Strike-through text, as in legal documents
_{...}	Subscript
^{...}	Superscript

In addition, HTML+ includes a <RENDER> markup tag for translations of elements from other SGML-based formats. The render tag goes in the head of the document and takes two attributes: a TAG attribute to define the name of the tag to be found in the document body, and a STYLE tag to instruct the browser on how to render the marked-up text. For example:

```
<RENDER TAG="HEADLINE" STYLE="B,U">
```

The STYLE attribute is a comma-separated list of style tag names from the following list: I, B, U, S, SUP, SUB, TT. The name, P, may also be included to instruct the browser to force paragraph breaks before and after the marked-up text.

Footnote (<FOOTNOTE></FOOTNOTE>) and margin (<MARGIN></MARGIN>) tags are provided in HTML+ to include annotations for providing additional comments on the main text. When printed out, these annotations appear at the bottom of the page or in the page margin, as their name implies. For online use, browsers may show the annotation by a hypertext button such as a superscripted symbol or icon, which, when clicked, reveals the annotation in a pop-up window. Footnotes and margins can contain text with emphasis and images, but not other markup such as paragraphs, lists, or tables.

Often it is desirable to have different text on the printed version of a page and the online page. Text enclosed by the tags <PRINTED></PRINTED> will appear only on the printed page, whereas text enclosed by the tags <ONLINE></ONLINE> will appear only on displays.

Figures are different than in-line images in that they may have captions. A figure is specified with the <FIG></FIG> tags. A caption for the figure is defined with the <CAPTION></CAPTION> tags placed right after the starting <FIG> tag. Any text following the caption is treated in the same manner as text assigned to the ALT attribute of the <IMG> tag. The ALIGN attribute can have a value of "left", "center", "right", or "float" to determine the position of the figure with respect to the page. Text following the ending figure tag flows around the image.

Tables are specified using <TABLE></TABLE> tags. Captions for tables are specified in the same manner as figures; however, table captions appear above the table, whereas figure captions appear below. Tables have header and data cells defined by the empty tags, <TH> and <TD>. Cells may contain text, paragraphs, lists, and headers. Each row of a table is ended by table row tag <TR>. For example, the following HTML code,

```
<TABLE>
<CAPTION>Example Table</CAPTION>
<TH>Col 1 <TH>Col 2 <TH>Col 3 <TR>
<TD>C1,R1 <TD>C2,R1 <TD>C3,R1 <TR>
```

```
<TD>C1,R2 <TD>C2,R2 <TD>C3,R2
</TABLE>
```

will define a 2-row-by-3-column table that might be rendered by an HTML+ browser as

Example Table

Col 1	Col 2	Col 3
C1,R1	C2,R1	C3,R1
C1,R2	C2,R2	C3,R2

Additional table attributes exist in HTML+ to define more complex tables, such as those with table headings that span multiple rows and columns, or tables with borders.

The specifications for the support of mathematical equations in HTML+ are still evolving. In general, the approach involves enclosing the expression with $$ markup tags to signal to the browser that special formatting is required. Within the expression standard ISO character entity names are used for mathematical symbols (*∫* for the integral symbol and *∞* for the infinity symbol). Elements are grouped with the <BOX> </BOX> and <ARRAY></ARRAY> markup tags, and expressions can be divided into numerator and denominator sets with the empty <OVER> tag.

HTML+ provides additional character entities as well as support for ISO standard entity names. Here are some of those additional entities:

&cent;	Cent sign
&pound;	Pound sign
&yen;	Yen sign
&brvbar;	Broken vertical bar
&sect;	Section sign
&copy;	Copyright sign
&laquo;	Angle quotation mark, left
&raquo;	Angle quotation mark, right
&not;	Negation sign
&reg;	Circled R, registered sign
&deg;	Degree sign

&plusmn;	Plus or minus sign
&sup1;	Superscript 1
&sup2;	Superscript 2
&sup3;	Superscript 3
&micro;	Micro sign
&para;	Paragraph sign
&middot;	Center dot
&frac14;	Fraction 1/4
&frac12;	Fraction 1/2
&frac34;	Fraction 3/4
&iquest;	Inverted question mark
&AElig;	capital AE diphthong (ligature)

NETSCAPE EXTENSIONS TO HTML

To the horizontal rule element, <HR>, Netscape has added new attributes to allow the document author some control over how the rule should look. The SIZE attribute specifies how thick the horizontal rule should be. The WIDTH attribute, which can be specified as either a number of pixels or a percent of the page, controls the length of the line. If the WIDTH attribute is used, the ALIGN attribute can be included to indicate that the rule be aligned "left", "right", or "center" with respect to the page.

To the Unordered list element, <UL>, Netscape has added a TYPE tag so you can specify whether you want a TYPE="disc", TYPE="circle", or TYPE="square" as the bullet. With the Ordered list element, <OL>, the TYPE attribute controls the marking with the following values: "A" for capital letters, "a" for small letters, "I" for large roman numerals, and "1" for the default of numbers. The START attribute can be used to start an ordered list at a value other than 1. START takes a number that is converted to the appropriate TYPE before display. The TYPE attribute can also be included in the list item tag, <LI>. It takes the same values as either UL or OL, depending on the type of list you are in, and it changes the list type for that item and all subsequent items.

Netscape has significantly extended the <IMG> tag. The ALIGN attribute has additional values, "left" and "right". Images with these alignments are an entirely new floating image type. An ALIGN="left" image will float down and over to the left margin (into the next available space there), and subsequent text will wrap around the right-hand side of that image. Likewise for ALIGN="right"; the image aligns with the right margin, and the text wraps around the left. WIDTH and HEIGHT attributes are added to IMG to speed up display of the document by providing the browser with information to pre-allocate space on the page before the image is moved over the network. Both attributes take a value that is a number of pixels. VSPACE and HSPACE are attributes for controlling the space around floating images.

With the addition of floating images, Netscape extended the line break tag, <BR>, with the CLEAR attribute. CLEAR="left" will break the line and move vertically down until there is a clear left margin (no floating images). CLEAR= "right" does the same for the right margin, and CLEAR="all" moves down the page until both margins are clear of images.

Netscape has two new elements, <NOBR></NOBR> and <WBR>, to help control line breaks in a paragraph. The NOBR element stands for *NO Break*; this means any white space between the start and end tags is treated as if it were the * * character entity. The WBR element stands for *Word Break*; this is for the very rare case in which you have a NOBR section and you know exactly where you want it to break. The WBR element does not force a line break (BR does that), it simply lets Netscape know where a line break can be inserted if needed.

Netscape has a FONT element that can take a SIZE attribute, as in <FONT-SIZE=5>...</FONT>. Valid values range from 1 to 7; the default font size is 3. The value given to size can optionally have a + or - character in front of it to specify that it is relative to the document base font.

Netscape has a CENTER element. All lines of text between the beginning and ending <CENTER> tags are centered between the current left and right margins.

Finally, Netscape has a BLINK element. All text between the beginning and ending <BLINK> tags are displayed by the Netscape browser with a blinking background.

Appendix C: Resources

I n this appendix are some resources that may be of use to you in developing documents for the World Wide Web.

HTML Guides and References

From CERN:

HyperText Markup Language
http://info.cern.ch/hypertext/WWW/MarkUp/MarkUp.html

Style Guide for Online Hypertext
http://info.cern.ch/hypertext/WWW/Provider/Style/Overview.html

HTML+ (Hypertext Markup Format)
http://info.cern.ch/hypertext/WWW/MarkUp/HTMLPlus/htmlplus_1.html

Uniform Resource Locators (URLs)
file://info.cern.ch/pub/www/doc/url-spec.txt

From NCSA:

A Beginner's Guide to HTML
http://www.ncsa.uiuc.edu/General/Internet/WWW/HTMLPrimer.html

Beginner's Guide to Uniform Resource Locators (URLs)
http://www.ncsa.uiuc.edu/demoweb/url-primer.html

Mosaic Fill-Out Form Support
http://www.ncsa.uiuc.edu/SDG/Software/Mosaic/Docs/fill-out-forms/
overview.html

The Common Gateway Interface
http://hoohoo.ncsa.uiuc.edu/cgi/overview.html

Technical Documentation from Dan Connolly:

HTML Specification Review Materials
http://www.hal.com/~connolly/html-spec/index.html

HTML Design Notebook
http://www.hal.com/~connolly/drafts/html-design.html

HTML DTD Reference
http://www.hal.com/~connolly/html-spec/L2Pindex.html

Other HTML documentation:

The HTML Developers' Jumpstation
http://oneworld.wa.com/htmldev/devpage/dev-page1.html

Hypermedia authoring tools
http://info.mcc.ac.uk/CGU/staff/lilley/authoring.html

Introduction to HTML Documentation
http://www.utirc.utoronto.ca/HTMLdocs/NewHTML/intro.html

Peter Flynn's "How to Write HTML"
http://kcgl1.eng.ohio-state.edu/www/doc/htmldoc.html

Ian Graham's Guide to HTML
http://www.utirc.utoronto.ca/HTMLdocs/NewHTML/htmlindex.html

WORLD WIDE WEB BROWSERS

The following list of browsers is adapted from CERN's Web page at http://info.cern.ch/hypertext/WWW/Clients.html. The URLs given for these products will provide additional information on the product and how to get it. New browsers are appearing every month. If you're not satisfied with your current World Wide Web client, the above URL is the place to check for alternatives.

Terminal-based browsers:

Line-Mode Browser (tty)
http://info.cern.ch/hypertext/WWW/LineMode/Status.html

"Lynx" Full-Screen Browser (vt100)
http://info.cern.ch/hypertext/WWW/Lynx/Status.html

Tom Fine's perlWWW
http://info.cern.ch/hypertext/WWW/FineWWW/Status.html

Slipknot from MicroMind (a Windows front end to Lynx and WWW)
ftp://oak.oakland.edu/SimTel/win3/internet/slnot100.zip

PC with Windows browsers:

Cello—from Cornell LII
http://www.law.cornell.edu/cello/cellotop.html

NCSA Mosaic for Windows
http://www.ncsa.uiuc.edu/SDG/Software/WinMosaic/HomePage.html

EINet's WinWeb
http://galaxy.einet.net/EINet/WinWeb/WinWebHome.html

GWHIS (commercial version of NCSA Mosaic from Quadralay Inc.)
http://www.quadralay.com/www/ProductInfo/gwhis/win/index.html

Netscape from Netscape Communications, Inc.
http://www.mcom.com/info/index.html

Enhanced Mosaic from Spyglass, Inc.
http://www.spyglass.com/mprodinf.htm

AirMosaic from Spry, Inc.
http://www.spry.com/sp_prod/airmos/airmos.html

InternetWorks from BookLink Technologies, Inc.
http://www.booklink.com/Press/default.htm

Macintosh browsers

NCSA Mosaic for Macintosh
http://www.ncsa.uiuc.edu/SDG/Software/MacMosaic/MacMosaicHome.html

Samba from CERN
http://info.cern.ch/hypertext/WWW/Macintosh/Status.html

EINet's MacWeb
http://galaxy.einet.net/EINet/MacWeb/MacWebHome.html

Enhanced Mosaic from Spyglass Inc.
http://www.spyglass.com/mprodinf.htm

Netscape from Netscape Communications, Inc.
http://www.mcom.com/info/index.html

X-Windows browsers:

NCSA Mosaic for X using X11/Motif
http://www.ncsa.uiuc.edu/SDG/Software/Mosaic/Docs/help-about.html

GWHIS Viewer for X from Quadralay, Inc.
http://www.quadralay.com/products/products.html

tkWWW Browser/Editor for X11
http://info.cern.ch/hypertext/WWW/TkWWW/Status.html

MidasWWW (browser from Tony Johnson)
http://info.cern.ch/hypertext/WWW/MidasWWW/Status.html

Chimera (browser using Athena)
http://www.unlv.edu/chimera/

Netscape from Netscape Communications, Inc.
http://www.mcom.com/info/index.html

Enhanced Mosaic from Spyglass, Inc.
http://www.spyglass.com/mprodinf.htm

VMS browsers:

Dudu Rashty's Full-Screen Client
http://info.cern.ch/hypertext/WWW/RashtyClient/Status.html

Emacs w3-mode
http://info.cern.ch/hypertext/WWW/EmacsWWW/Status.html

Browsers for other platforms:

IBM's Web Explorer for OS/2 Warp
http://www.austin.ibm.com/pspinfo/product0.html

A browser/editor for NeXTStep
http://info.cern.ch/hypertext/WWW/NextStep/Status.html

Albert for VM systems (by David Nessl)
ftp://www.ufl.edu/pub/vm/www/README

HTML editing tools

HTML editors for Windows:

HoTMetaL for Windows(a commercial HTML editor by SoftQuad)
http://www.sq.com/

HTML Assistant (a Windows HTML editor by Howard Harawitz)
ftp://ftp.cs.dal.ca/htmlasst/htmlafaq.htm

html-helper-mode (for use with emacs, by Nelson Minar)
http://www.reed.edu/~nelson/tools/

HTML Writer (by Kris Nosack)
ftp://lal.cs.byu.edu/pub/www/tools/htmlwrit.zip

HTML editors for Macintosh:

HTML Editor for Macintosh (by Rich Giles)
http://dragon.acadiau.ca:1667/~giles/HTML_Editor

BBEdit HTML Extensions (by Carles Bellver)
http://www.uji.es/bbedit-html-extensions.html

Simple HTML Editor (a Hypercard-based editor)
http://dewey.lib.ncsu.edu/staff/morgan/simple.html

HTML editors for X Windows:

TkWWW (Tk/Tcl-based WWW browser/editor)
ftp://info.cern.ch:/pub/www/dev/

tkHTML (a near-WYSWYG editor based on Tk/Tcl)
http://alfred1.u.washington.edu:8080/~roland/tkHTML/tkHTML.html

HoTMetaL for SUN from SoftQuad
http://www.sq.com/

HTML Conversion Tools

There's a large and growing number of tools available to assist the HTML author in converting documents from various word processor and text editor formats. The sites listed below maintain good descriptive lists of many of these tools.

http://info.cern.ch/hypertext/WWW/Tools/

http://www.utirc.utoronto.ca/HTMLdocs/pc_tools.html

http://cbl.leeds.ac.uk/nikos/doc/repository.html

ftp://src.doc.ic.ac.uk/computing/information-systems/www/tools/translators/

OTHER WORLD WIDE WEB–RELATED RESOURCES

To subscribe to any of the mailing lists below, send an e-mail message to <listserv@info.cern.ch> with the following in the body of the message:

```
subscribe <listname> <your_name>
```

where *listname* is one of the five choices below and *your_name* is your full name. For example:

```
subscribe www-html John Public
```

Any information in the subject field will be ignored. Also, be sure that no signature information is attached to the message, as this will generate an error.

News groups:

comp.infosystems.www.users	For Browser issues
comp.infosystems.www.providers	For Server issues
comp.infosystems.www.misc	For anything else
comp.infosystems.announce	For announcements

Mailing lists:

www-announce	Announcements of new Web sites and products
www-html	Issues relating to the HTML language
www-proxy	Issues relating to the use of proxy servers
www-talk	Technical issues relating to the Web
www-rdb	The Web and relational databases

Index